MY CHILD
DREAM

A DREAM I JUST COULDN'T LET GO OF

DENNIS EDENFIELD

outskirts
press

Preface

At the age of 19, I stepped aboard a Greyhound bus in my hometown of New Orleans and headed for New York City. My childhood dreams of performing on Broadway had begun. Just like in the movies!

When I published my professional website I wrote an introduction on the home page. When I went back to read what I had just written, it suddenly occurred to me that I just wrote the first paragraph to my (someday-to-be) memoir. Before I take you on this journey of my life, I will share some things about my childhood that put me on that Greyhound bus to New York.

Introduction

WHEN I DECIDED to venture into this process of writing my memoir, I also made the decision that I would write about what influenced me and encouraged me to chase my dream, and how this dream of a career in show business grabbed me by the heart and wouldn't let go. My motivation for writing this was to share my journey and offer some inspiration to others who may have their own dream, whether it's to have a career in show business or a dream of becoming an astronaut.

To all those I crossed paths with during my life and have not mentioned in this book, please understand that my focus was strictly on my career development and not my personal private life, with a few exceptions. Nor did I want to invade anyone's privacy.

Many thanks to my friend, Muriel Faxon, for her time spent editing the first draft. A special thanks to David for his undying support and attention in lending his help. I also want to express my gratitude to those who encouraged me to write this book and share my life with you, the readers.

Dedication

A deepfelt love to you, John, who came into my life all too briefly, only to leave prematurely.

And a deep-felt love to you, David, who came into my life when I needed you most and helped me heal, and now shares my life as if you were always here.

I am grateful to my friend Ted Landry for his time editing and encouraging me to pursue the publishing of this book.

Table of Contents

CHAPTER 1

I Was Always a Show-Off

IF I SAW it on TV, I could do it. One of my favorite Saturday morning shows was *The Big Top Circus*. One Saturday there was an act with a tightrope walker. Of course, I tried to make a tightrope in our backyard. I couldn't make the rope tight enough, so I never was able to walk it. Then there was a trapeze act, so I made a trapeze hanging from a tree and I actually was able to swing by my legs. That was fun. What wasn't fun was when I tried to do an arabesque on my bicycle. As I glided down the street, I stood on top of my bicycle seat on one leg and lifted the other leg up behind me. Then all of a sudden I lost my balance and fell on top of the bike and ended up impaling my thigh onto the rod of the broken bicycle pedal. My momma got our neighbor to drive us to a nearby medical clinic. I remember lying on Momma's lap in the backseat of the neighbor's car crying, "Am I going to die?" I received twenty stitches. This clinic was a place she would take me to often as I was always hurting myself. One day I decided to swing on the clothesline T-bar. I was doing pretty well until I swung all the way around the bar and lost my grip, landing flat on the concrete. You guessed it: back to the clinic for more stitches. My poor momma had her hands full with me and my two brothers.

In New Orleans, there is a recreational program similar to the YMCA called NORD, New Orleans Recreation Department. At the beginning of summer, there was a TV show about the different programs NORD was offering for free. "Free" being the operative word as we were a lower-income family. One of the programs was tumbling. As I watched some of the kids on TV do their tricks, I thought, *I can do that*. I always thought I could do anything I wanted to do. So after the TV show, my momma saw me in the yard trying to do a back somersault. She yelled out the window, "Stop, please stop before you break your neck!" I always did as my momma said ... sometimes. The next day she took me to the NORD playground to start my first tumbling class. It turned out that I was a natural. I took two classes a week and would practice at home on the front lawn—I liked having an audience.

About six months into my tumbling lessons, at the age of eight, I won first place in the New Orleans City Championship Games. That's when my tumbling teacher suggested that my parents take me to study with Mr. Lee Early, the best tumbling teacher in New Orleans. At that time I had no idea how tumbling would be a huge benefit to my theatrical career. As a matter of fact, at that time, I didn't know I was going to have a theatrical career.

I can remember like it was yesterday one steamy summer night when my momma was ironing our clothes and watching the *Late Night Movie* on TV. Momma would iron later in the evening because we were all in bed and it was cooler. We didn't have air-conditioning so we would open all the windows, and with the window fan on there was a gentle breeze. From the bedroom that I shared with my two brothers, Timmy and Randy, I could faintly hear Judy Garland singing on the TV. My momma loved her and loved singing along with Judy. Momma had a really good voice. As I often did, I crawled into the dark hallway where I could see the TV. Momma was watching an old movie called *For Me and My Gal,* starring Judy Garland. It took place during the vaudeville days of live entertainment. This was the first time I saw Gene Kelly dance. Actually, it was his first movie. As I watched him dance, I could feel his movement with the music. His dancing was mesmerizing. Gene Kelly could do back somersaults like me. I became obsessed with Mr. Kelly's dancing and I would pray every night that someday I could dance like him. Eventually, my momma, knowing I was in the hallway, said I could come into the living room and watch with her. As I watched the movie, I had this strange feeling that I had been there in another lifetime. I didn't even know what that meant. Somehow, I just knew I had been in vaudeville. Weird! It will be a few years before it becomes apparent that I was born to be in show business. I guess it was hereditary.

My momma had a great voice, and my Aunt Dede, who raised Momma, was a fabulous entertainer. When my momma was three, her mother Corrine LeCorgne Kelly unexpectedly died, leaving two young sons and two young daughters. Momma's father Harry Kelly kept the boys to raise and the girls would go to the sisters, Aunt Dede and Aunt Adele. Aunt Dede, whose real name was Mercedes, asked if she could raise little Margie, my momma. Mercedes would eventually marry and give birth to Brenda, who would be my godmother when I was born. Aunt Dede's marriage would end in divorce.

Now alone with two young girls to support, Aunt Dede took a job at McCrory's, a favorite dime store in New Orleans. Aunt Dede would play from sheet music on the piano in hopes that the customers would then buy the music. She also played commercials on the radio. Her big break came when she was offered a job at Pat O'Brien's, a small bar in New Orleans' French Quarter. As Mercedes' popularity grew, so did Pat O'Brien's bar. Not only did Pat O'Brien's have Mercedes, they also had a specialty cocktail called the Hurricane. This cocktail is a wonderful fruit punch concoction with dark and white rum, then served over chipped ice in a tall glass shaped like an old-fashioned hurricane lantern. With Mercedes at the piano and the Hurricane on the bar, Pat O'Brien's became one of the most popular bars in the French Quarter.

Mercedes was well known all over New Orleans and remembered by all the many tourists and Hollywood celebrities who visited the Crescent City. Now at war, the country's Second World War, Mercedes did her part to help keep morale up. She entertained at many U.S.O. shows, going from camp to camp. She was beloved by the many soldiers who, when on leave, would visit New Orleans and Pat's to see their beloved Mercedes. In a biography written by Fanny B. Campbell Whelsh titled *Mercedes: A New Orleans Hurricane*, I read that a war blimp was named *Mercedes of New Orleans* and several military pilots had "MERCEDES" painted on the side of their planes. But as a kid growing up in New Orleans, she was just Aunt Dede to me.

Family at Pat O'Brien's
Starting on the left: my godmother Brenda, her husband Fred, my daddy,
Aunt Dede, not sure who is next, and my momma on the far right.

I was probably nine years old when my class at school took a field trip to see a touring company perform a musical version of *Hansel and Gretel*. I had never been to a theatre to see a play. As I looked around, I realized that the theatre was packed with other schoolkids. As we took our seats, the lights started to dim and the orchestra started playing music—now I know it was the overture. As the music ended the curtain went up, and the lights revealed a beautiful stage set that looked like a real village. There were actors in costumes singing and dancing. As I watched the show, I wanted to be up on stage singing and dancing with the others. This is when I knew I was destined to spend my life on stage.

In 1957, my momma had to take a job outside of the home. She worked part-time at the dry cleaners on Highway 90, just a couple of blocks from our house. Up till then, she was like many other mothers who were stay-at-home moms. My momma cooked three meals a day from scratch, cleaned the house, washed our clothes, and shopped for our food. My daddy also worked hard. He was a butcher and worked long hours six days a week, and on Sunday he worked half a day. With Momma working now I would come home after school and wait for my little brother Randy, who was six, to get off the school bus. I was the eleven-year-old babysitter. After school I would make Randy a peanut-butter-and-jelly sandwich with a glass of milk. Randy would watch his favorite cartoon show, *The Yogi Bear Show*, which really made him giggle—a lot. Then we would walk up the street to the dry cleaners where Momma worked. We would hang out with her for a while, and then I would walk Randy back home. At some point, Momma would call on the phone and give me instructions on starting dinner and then call back later to check on how things were going and give more instructions. When she got off work, she would come home and take over the cooking. Basically, this is how I learned to cook.

CHAPTER 2

Tumbling and a Garage Theatre

AS A STUDENT of Mr. Early, I continued to advance in hurling my body into the air and twisting and somersaulting before successfully landing on my feet and not my head. Mr. Early taught me how to successfully execute a layout back somersault. I could already do a back somersault, which is accomplished by tucking the knees to the chest, thus helping the body spin 360 degrees quickly so you land on your feet. A layout back somersault is executed by not tucking the knees into the chest; instead, as you throw your body up in the air, you lie back into the spin and straighten the body like a board. This slows down the speed of the body, giving you the feeling of flying. It's an incredible experience.

Most dancing schools did teach acrobatics but not tumbling—a big difference—so Mr. Early was invited to bring some of his students to perform a number in the dancing schools' revues. Mr. Early would choreograph a dance number around our tumbling. Well, I did not, at that time, have any dance training like the others in my class. Also, I was a little dyslectic, which attributed to my being slow at learning and remembering the dance steps. Mr. Early really wanted to use my tumbling in the numbers so he would have me wait in the wings until it was time for me to do a tumbling pass across the stage. This was frustrating because I really wanted to dance with the others. I still wanted to dance like Gene Kelly. Mr. Early used to tease me by calling me Pavlova. Who is Pavlova? At that time, I didn't know who Pavlova was, and I'm sure Mr. Early didn't know he was hurting my feelings.

When I was in the third grade, our tumbling class was invited to appear on the original *Today Show* on NBC with host Dave Garroway. The show was touring the big cities in the country. It was very exciting to me because it would be my first time on television, albeit brief. Each of us only got to do one tumbling pass. Even at that age I was pissed because we had to get up real early to get to the studio. Mr. Early's class was also invited to be a part of the entertainment in some of the Mardi Gras Balls, which started after the new year and lasted until Mardi Gras day. These balls were large and very elegant. Formal attire only. Most were held at the Municipal Auditorium. The auditorium was huge and could be converted into back-to-back proscenium stages or one could lower the stages to the floor level and open up the entire auditorium to one huge arena. We did an incredible musical number in one of these balls. We wore red body tights with a hood that had the devil's horns. We also had a devil's tail. We were little devils with Mr. Early as the Master Devil. At the beginning of the music—Mr. Early used "The Sabre Dance"—the lights changed to red and a section of the center floor opened up so this big cauldron could rise up from the basement, Hell, to the arena floor. There was stage smoke coming from the fake fire under the cauldron. The Master Devil was standing in the middle of us cracking his whip as we did tumbling passes around the cauldron. It was an exciting production number. I think we got a standing ovation. If not, we should have, *damn it!*

Momma going to a Mardi Gras Ball

Momma going to a Mardi Gras Ball. The gown was a hand-me-down from Aunt Dede, which Momma redesigned. Notice the tiara that Momma made along with the belt.

Disney's *The Mickey Mouse Club* was a very popular after-school television show that aired on Monday through Friday. Every day it had a different theme. I believe it was on a Friday that a short serial titled *Spin and Marty* would air. There was this particular episode that was about the Mouseketeers going to a dude ranch. They were going to put on a show to raise money for something or other. So they decided to turn an old barn into a theatre, just like in the Gene Kelly and Judy Garland movie *Summer Stock*. It was fascinating to watch the process of building a theatre in a barn. To this day I can't look at a barn without pondering if this barn could become a theatre. Well this really interested me. I just had to do this but I didn't have a barn—but wait, I did have a garage, hmm!

I spent a lot of time in the library researching books on how to make stage curtains, how they were rigged, and how to create scenery and stage lights. I took a couple of patch-quilt blankets out of the closet to make curtains. I took Christmas lights and hung them from the rafters. I brought the portable record player out to the garage theatre so I could have music. I loved this idea of building a theatre and putting on shows. A neighbor's grandson wanted to also put on shows, and a couple of blocks down the road there were two sisters who wanted to play theatre with us. Once we got the Christmas lights hung from the beams and the blanket curtains working where they actually opened and closed, we then put together a show where we would lip-sync to show albums. We told some of the neighborhood about our upcoming show, and nobody showed up. So the theatre garage quickly became just a garage again.

CHAPTER 3

Junior High, Cheerleading, the Saturday Hop, and Dance Lessons

IN 1959, I entered Colton Junior High School. Here is where the tumbling comes into play. I was encouraged to audition to be a cheerleader because of my tumbling ability. I did try out and became the first male cheerleader, I think, at Colton Junior High. Of course, there was some name-calling, which really hurt my feelings, and after a while the name-calling wasn't as mean. Some would call me "rubber legs," which was better than what they used to call me. They called me rubber legs because when I tumbled, I was able to jump really high in the air to do back somersaults, hence my legs were made of rubber.

I was on stage a lot at Colton. My English teacher, who did summer stock, taught an acting course. The teacher would choose a play, and we would rehearse for weeks and then perform the play for the entire school. Along with the plays, Colton Junior High also presented the Spring Festival every April. This was a big deal because almost anyone could participate. I got to perform in several musical numbers. In one of the festivals I was picked to sing and do a soft-shoe to the song "Harrigan" by George M. Cohan. By the way, whenever I needed a costume, which was often, Momma would make all of them. "Harrigan" is a soft-shoe tempo. I didn't know how to do a soft-shoe but my friend Wayne, who was part of the Garage Theatre failed project, did know how and he taught me. I also did a Charleston number from *The Boyfriend* in another Spring Festival. The Spring Festival played for two performances—one in the day for the school and one in the evening for the paying audience, like family and friends and whoever would buy a ticket.

I liked going to school. My grades were a little higher than average and I participated in many after-school activities. These activities were my incentive to get me out of bed in the morning There would be rehearsals for the shows and cheerleader practice. I was a member of the Choir and the Newman Club, which has a focus on Catholicism. I was the treasurer. I was honored with The Newman Club Award. The ceremony was held at a beautiful cathedral, I don't remember the name. I do remember in the ceremony the Archbishop spoke of the blessing of being chosen to serve God as a priest or nun. At some point I had to kiss the Archbishop's ring. After the ceremonial event I remember walking to our car and thinking to myself, *I like his robes and I always want to be chosen.* When we reached the car I said to Momma, "I think I will join the priesthood after graduation." She responded with, "That would be a wonderful thing to do but priests don't make a lot of money. Remember, you promised me that when you become a big star you will buy me a mink coat and a big house with a maid and pool." I gave it a quick thought and said, "I think I would rather be a star."

When I was in the eighth grade at Colton I started dating and going to the school dances. I would always buy my date a corsage, like Momma said. Then in 1960 a T.V. show, *Saturday Saturday Hop*, debuted in New Orleans. *Saturday Hop* was like *American Band Stand* hosted by Dick Clark. If you wanted to be on *Saturday Hop*, you and your date had to be in the lobby of the T.V studio a half hour before the show aired. The host, John Pela, would come into the lobby and pick several couples to be on the show and dance to all the hit songs of the week. I started going to *Saturday Hop* every Saturday and my date and I were always picked.

One of the girls that I was dating in school was taking dance lessons at The Emma Pembo School of Dance. Sometimes I would walk with her to the dancing school and watch class. One day I said to my parents that I really wanted to take dancing lessons. My daddy said no, we couldn't afford it. I said that I would give up my tumbling lessons to pay for the dancing lessons; he still said "*no!*" I knew in the back of my mind that he thought only a sissy would take dancing lessons.

Then a lucky break happened. Miss Emma told me that if I would clean her studio on Sundays, when it was closed, I could take lessons for free. I couldn't wait to tell my momma. I don't remember how long it took me to tell my daddy, if ever. So now I was taking dancing lessons. I liked going and really liked Miss Emma. I shared my dream of dancing on Broadway with her and she was very supportive.

The National Dance Convention was coming to New Orleans. This was a big deal! It was a three-day event with a faculty of several famous dance teachers and choreographers on the program. The convention featured Robert Joffrey from The Joffrey Ballet, Ernie Flatt, then choreographer of *The Gary Moore Show* and later the *Carol Burnett Show*, and Bob Audy, who several years later would give me my first professional job in summer stock. Mr. Joffrey taught ballet classes, Mr. Flatt taught us a dance number from one of the TV shows, and Mr. Audy taught tap and jazz. The whole experience made me feel more confident about going to New York. At the end of the convention, I told Mr. Audy that I was going to New York after I graduated from high school. He said he choreographed summer stock every year and I should audition for him when I got to New York.

CHAPTER 4

1962: Good News and Summer on the Farm

IN THE SPRING, my grandma Kelly told my momma about an article she'd read regarding NORD having auditions for the musical *Good News*. I saw the movie starring June Allyson and Peter Lawford. It had some great dance numbers. So I did audition, and I was cast in a small role. It was exciting not to be performing in my garage but in a theatre, albeit a small theatre, and with other talented people. Some are still my friends today. I loved the rehearsal process, learning the dancing and singing. On the opening night, there was a party after the show, and around 11 p.m. the director went across the park to the newspaper office to get the review. It was a good review—*Yay!* When the show closed, we were off to Florida for the rest of the summer. It was a family tradition that we would go to Grandma and Poppa Edenfield's farm for the summer. On a Friday night after work, Daddy and Momma would pack us into the car, and we drove all night to arrive at the Edenfield farm the next morning. Back then, there were no interstate highways, so it took about eight hours to get there. Daddy could only stay overnight. Then he would drive back to New Orleans on Sunday night so he could be at work on Monday morning. The farm was in the panhandle of Florida near the Alabama and Georgia borders and way out in the country. As a small child I didn't like it much.

The side porch and smokehouse in back.   **Me on the front porch.**

The farmhouse was old and had a tin roof and no ceilings overhead. The only water was the spigot outside on the kitchen porch or at the well out front. Oh yes, no indoor bathroom, just an outhouse near the barn. Grandma had a potty in her bedroom, but only for the females. The males had to pee off the back porch at night. No one would use the outhouse after dark. On the kitchen porch, there was a big bucket; it was called the "slop bucket" where the leftover food of the day would end up. That was the pigs' dinner and we kids got to feed the pigs, which was called "slopping the pigs."

I enjoyed all the animals on the farm, like the cows and chickens and pigs. I vaguely remember trying to milk a cow but don't remember how that turned out. I did help with churning the fresh cream into butter. Grandma had lots of chickens. I liked collecting the eggs. The chickens were pretty much cage-free, so they would nest under the house and out in the barn or wherever. And there were many pigs and always baby piglets, which we kids got to name. We had lots of watermelons all summer. The older boys were allowed to drive the tractor, with a long wagon, out to the field and pick some watermelon. When the wagon was not being used to bring in the watermelon, corn, and sugar cane from the fields, I used the wagon as a stage. I would place my transistor radio on the wagon and sing along with Elvis, Paul Anka, Ricky Nelson, and even Connie Francis. I used a corncob as my microphone.

When we ate the watermelon, we would sit on the edge of the porch and spit the seeds in the yard. In the south we sprinkle a pinch of salt on our fruits, especially watermelons. The salt would bring out the sweetness of the fruit and make it juicier.

Grandma, like most people in the south, had a hand-crank ice-cream maker. If you have never seen an old-fashioned ice-cream maker, there is a round silver cylinder where you poured the cream mixture in and the cylinder would fit inside of the wooden bucket. Then the bucket was filled to the brim with chopped ice and then covered with rock salt. Then you covered the ice-cream maker with burlap sacks. Someone would have to sit on the ice-cream maker and someone would crank the handle. It took a while, but it was well worth the effort. The result was delicious homemade ice cream. Sometimes we would have peach ice cream with peaches that Aunt Inez brought down from Georgia. There is this great swimming place called Blue Springs. It was a beautiful spot. The springs were surrounded by cypress trees and these majestic oaks with Spanish moss. It was a popular picnic spot. The springs would rush out from an underground cave into this huge pond. The water was crystal clear and was the coldest water I have ever felt. People would put their watermelons in the water to make them cold. There was a diving board on a platform right over the springs, and I loved to show off by diving and doing somersaults off the board. There was this shack-like building where we could buy hamburgers, hotdogs, and shakes. There was a jukebox of course, and I would show off by dancing with all the girls.

Meanwhile, back at the farm, I loved watching Grandma and Momma cook in the kitchen. Grandma did have an icebox, but food left over from breakfast and lunch, like cornbread, biscuits, or anything that didn't require refrigeration, was kept in the Hoosier cabinet away from the flies and served at supper. To this day I still catch myself calling the fridge the icebox.

CHAPTER 5

Nicholls High School, Community Theatre, and Ballet Class

HIGH SCHOOL WAS a very different experience for me compared to junior high. I decided not to audition for cheerleader. I wanted to focus on my dance classes and get more involved with the community theatres. When I was in the tenth grade I did another show at the NORD theatre, *Annie Get Your Gun*. I talked my best friend Augie into auditioning and he was cast. I had the small role of the Ceremonial Dancer and I got my first mention in the critic's review. When I was in the 11th grade, I heard that a community theatre in the French Quarter, Gallery Circle, was having auditions for a production of *My Fair Lady*. So I auditioned, and I was cast. The choreographer was Gayle Parmelee. She had been a very successful dancer on Broadway, dancing in *Oklahoma* and *Silk Stockings*, and she was also a Rockette at The Radio Music Hall. After the show closed, I began studying ballet at Gaye's studio. She also created the ballet company Ballet de Nouvelle Orléans.

I told two friends of mine who were in the school choir with me about the auditions for *My Fair Lady*; both had beautiful voices, and both were cast in leading roles. Barbara Bollinger was cast as Eliza, and Henry Hitt was cast as Freddie. I was cast in a small part, one of the Cockneys who sang "Wouldn't It Be Loverly" with Eliza, and I was also in the chorus. That Christmas we got our first stereo console record player. It came with a bonus of three albums, and Momma let us boys pick an album. I picked *My Fair Lady*. I used this album to learn how to speak without an accent. My momma had a distinct New Orleans accent and my daddy had a country accent.

When the show closed, I started to study ballet at Gail's studio. I would ride the bus all the way across town to the Garden District, the opposite end of New Orleans from where I lived and went to school. It took me a long time to get there, and I didn't mind. I took class after school and on Saturdays. The summer before I would leave for New York, Gayle cast me in the ballet *Diana and Actaeon*. I was honored to dance the role of Actaeon. This was performed with The Mississippi Coast Ballet. I also danced the role of Aeneas in *Dido and Aeneas*. We performed in Dixon Hall on the campus of Tulane University, where I had a part-time job in the library.

This is me dancing the role of Actaeon in the ballet *Diana and Actaeon*.

At Gayle's studio a new teacher, Jack Payne, began teaching modern jazz classes. Modern jazz was a style of dance influenced by Jerome Robbins, Jack Cole, and Bob Fosse. I was invited to join the class. Jack was also a Broadway "gypsy," having danced on Broadway for Bob Fosse. Oh yes, a gypsy is a performer who goes from one show after another. I loved Jack's style and adapted to it quickly. So now I am dancing a lot and loving it. In the spring of 1964, Jack choreographed *How to Succeed in Business Without Really Trying* at Gallery Circle. Of course, I danced in the show. Between Gayle and Jack's mentoring I was learning all about New York and the theatre community. What to do and not to do at auditions. I lived and breathed musicals. I started taking the local bus downtown to the library where I would check out an album, remember the songs of a Broadway musical, and the book or libretto of the play. I would absorb them like a sponge. I would also go to the library at my high school and would peruse the *New York Times* Sunday's Entertainment section. I could see all the Broadway show ads and who was in these shows. There were also interesting articles about what was going on in the Broadway community. *West Side Story* finally arrived in the movie theatre in New Orleans. The first time I saw the movie, I stayed and watched it again. I knew then that I could dance like those boys on the screen. My daddy couldn't call any of these dancers sissy. Some of the dancers would become friends later in my life. When I got to New York I would take dance class from a few of them. I probably saw this movie a hundred times! I did see it enough times that I could remember most of the choreography.

In 1964, I also did *Guys and Dolls*. This was at Le Petit du Vieux Carré (the little old square). Located in the French Quarter, it is one of the oldest community theatres in the country. It is a beautiful theatre that received a multimillion-dollar renovation in 2012–13. It is designed in the Spanish Colonial style and seats 400-plus and is located across the street from the famous Jackson Square and St. Louis Cathedral. *Guys and Dolls* was a great show directed by Stocker Fontelieu and choreographed by Ivy McGee. Stocker was an excellent professional director who had been the artistic director for years. He was a sophisticated Frenchman, and I hung on to his every word. The cast was terrific and very talented. I am still friends with several of the cast members, like Ronald Murray, Joe Tremaine, and Sandy Trappey, who would be my dance partner in *The Pajama Game*—the next show at Le Petit in the summer of 1965. The costumes and sets at Le Petit were very professional and there was a ten-piece orchestra. I was unfamiliar with *Guys and Dolls*, unlike some of the other musicals. In dress rehearsal, I wanted to see the "Take Back Your Mink" number. Because only the girls were in this number, the guys were not called to rehearsal when they learned the "Take Back Your Mink" number. I was up in the balcony watching this sweet song and dance when all of a sudden the music changed tone and tempo, and the girls sang "Take back your mink" and threw their mink stoles on the floor, then "Take back your pearls" and they threw their pearls on the floor. They continued to sing "What made you think that I was one of those girls," then "Take back the gown," and they ripped off their gowns and on the floor the gowns went, leaving the girls standing there in their merry widows and black fishnet stockings. It was very hot! Especially to an 18-year-old boy who was still a virgin.

GUYS AND DOLLS

THE "HAVANA" NUMBER	CRAP SHOOTERS BALLET
I'm on the far right.	That is me in the center, second from the left.

THE PAJAMA GAME
I am center front with Sandy Trappey on my shoulder.

CHAPTER 6

1964: *The Ted Mack Amateur Hour,* High School Graduation, and a Big Bad Hurricane Named Betsy

REMEMBER *THE TED Mack Amateur Hour?* If you were born after 1965, probably not. It was this TV show in the '50s and '60s and the predecessor of shows like *Star Search* and *American Idol.* Many stars got their start on *The Ted Mack Amateur Hour,* such as Frank Sinatra, Ann-Margret, Pat Boone, and Gladys Knight, to name a few.

In 1964, the show was going through the south auditioning future talent. When they were in New Orleans, I thought "what the heck" so I did the audition. There must have been hundreds of people who auditioned. And the only reason I wanted to be on the show was to get a free plane ticket to New York City, and then I would just stay in New York and audition and get cast in a Broadway show. That was my plan. All of the people who auditioned had music and a routine—I didn't. I did tumble and improvised some dancing. I had only been studying ballet for a year and ballet and tumbling didn't go together. Modern jazz and tumbling do go together, but I had only been studying jazz dance for a few months so I had a limited repertoire of dance steps. I guess they liked what I did because a week after the audition the *Ted Mack Show* called my momma. They selected me to be on the show. I was so excited—New York City, here I come! Momma asked if I needed to bring music and they said that the music director would find something for me. Then I heard my momma say "Miami." Miami? As it turned out they were shooting in Miami that summer, not New York. So much for my plan to get a free trip to New York. Oh well, I would get to New York someday.

Unfortunately, I did not receive my music before I left for Miami so I wasn't able to set the whole routine. Oh yes, this would be my first ride in an airplane, let alone a jet. I remember asking the stewardess where my parachute was; she laughed. She must have thought I was a real "hick." When I arrived, I was taken to my hotel to check in—my first time staying in a hotel—and then to the theatre to rehearse before the taping of the show in the afternoon. The theatre was The Jackie Gleason Theatre, where he taped his show. They had chosen "Java" by Al Hirt for me to perform with. It was a big hit at the time, and I knew the music so I could work on my routine out in the hall. Before the show started there was a rehearsal with the orchestra, so I did get to hear my music played; however, I only heard it once and couldn't remember how many bars of music I had to use for my routine.

Later that afternoon before the show started, I had to go to the makeup room. I was used to putting my own makeup on, but in television the makeup was different from stage makeup so they had professional makeup artists. When the show went on the air and I heard Ted Mack starting his introduction to me, I thought I was going to pee in my pants. I still, to this day, have that problem with stage fright. Then the music started and so did I. I thought to myself, I will just tumble and dance as long as the music was playing. Well, the music kept going on and on. The conductor was waiting for me to finish and I was waiting for him to finish. I didn't think I would make it to the end, my heart was beating so hard. Finally I went down on one knee, throwing my arms up over my head in a pose, and the orchestra played a final chord of music ending my number. The show aired a couple of months later on a Sunday afternoon. With the family gathered around the TV, I watched intently and decided that, considering I was improvising most of the routine, I did a pretty good job, even though I didn't win. The winner was chosen by postcards. I guess we should have sent in more postcards.

Near the end of May, the national tour of *Hello Dolly*, starring Mary Martin and directed and choreographed by Gower Champion, came to New Orleans and played at the Municipal Auditorium. I had the opportunity to usher the performances. In return I received two free tickets, which I gave to Momma and Grandma Kelly. They loved Mary Martin and the show. As I watched each incredible performance, I would pray that someday I would dance in this show. Little did I know that in just fourteen months I would be hired by Gower Champion to join this very company of *Hello Dolly*, but with Betty Grable as Dolly.

In June of 1965, I graduated from high school. That summer was the first time I did not go to Florida with the family. Instead, I did *The Pajama Game* at Le Petit Theatre. It was directed by Stocker and choreographed by Diane Lazzar. I had a small part and sang and danced in the chorus. I was featured in the "Steam Heat" number with Trip Olino and Maxine McGee. There were only three dancers in "Steam Heat," and it was a great Bob Fosse number. Bob Fosse choreographed the Broadway production. The cast was fabulous as was the orchestra.

On the last performance of *The Pajama Game*, there was a closing night party, which is a tradition in the theatre like an opening night party, only somewhat sad. Someone put the *West Side Story* album on the record player and house speaker and I performed every dance on stage—yes, I am still a show-off. That night Stocker told me he was going to do *West Side Story* next summer. I didn't have the heart to tell him that I was moving to New York in April and wouldn't be able to be in the show. There was an after-party party. Knowing that it would probably last early into the morning, I called home and told Momma that I would probably stay in the Quarter at Jack and Bill's apartment because the bus would no longer be in service. The after-party did last until the early morning and I didn't stay at Jack and Bill's. Instead, when I woke up I found myself in a strange bed and, surprise, no longer a virgin.

After I graduated from high school, I got a job at the Whitney National Bank near the Quarter so I could go to rehearsals after work. I started saving money for my move to New York. My parents gave me a one-hundred-dollar bill in an envelope for my graduation. This was to help start up my savings account for my trip to New York. In September, New Orleans was hit badly by Hurricane Betsy. We'd experienced many hurricanes but this was the first time we had to evacuate. We drove to the meat-packing plant where Daddy worked. Because the building was a four-story concrete block building, Daddy thought we would be safer there, and we were. After the storm left New Orleans we were able to drive to Grandma Kelly's house. Out in the area where we lived, it was flooded with five feet of water. Finally, a couple of days later when the flood had subsided, we were able to go home. As we drove up to our house, we could see how badly damaged our home was, and when we went inside and saw all the sand and mud that covered the floors and the furniture plus the other damage, my momma broke down and cried. At least we didn't lose our home, and we were able to clean up the mess that Hurricane Betsy left us.

At the end of the summer WDSU, a New Orleans NBC TV station, aired *Critic's Call: Local Stars* with Al Shea. Mr. Shea saw three local productions of three musicals and picked three performers whom he felt deserved special mention. I was one of the three. He was kind enough to mail me a copy of his review that he read on the air. I still have that copy today. I have chosen not to post it to this page because it is very faded now and unreadable, so I have typed his critique:

In this month alone I've seen three local performers who if it were in my control I would see to it that New York or Hollywood or where ever it is talented people go nowadays knew about them. These three people are special for they possess that X factor called "Star Material." Not because they are particularly handsome or beautiful, not because they all sing, dance, act, or juggle, but because they have that undefinable knack called "Audience Appeal." When they are on stage, you look at no one else and not because they are busy or distracting, not at all. I loathe actors like that and I'm quick to unmask such tricks. No, Dennis Edenfield of Le Petit's The Pajama Game, *Philip McCoy of Gallery Circle's* A Funny Thing Happened on the Way to the Forum, *and Dee Kelly of Nord's* High Spirits *all have unquestionable good taste and natural ability. Mr. Edenfield in* Pajama Game *had perhaps six lines, he was merely a dancer in a chorus of good dancers, but his stage presence, his ability to make every movement like an explosion, as if it were truly happening for the first time, stood him atop of a line of expert dancers. (Mr. Shea goes on to describe how talented Philip McCoy and Dee Kelly are and ends his critique with this:) ... actors like Dee Kelly, Dennis Edenfield and Philip McCoy are talents who could meet and match the best that Broadway now has to offer and it is doubly nice when you think they're all local folks who are making good right here in the Crescent City.*

The "Steam Heat" number. I'm on the right.

CHAPTER 7

Finally, the Big Day
Had Arrived

THE MORNING OF April 3, 1966, was a bright spring day in New Orleans. I had spent the night before packing a footlocker that my momma had bought for my move to New York City. Along with my clothes my momma added to the footlocker a small tin pot—not for cooking, it was so I could put my Big Ben alarm clock in it. The idea was to make the alarm even louder. You see I was always hard to wake up in the mornings. This way I could get to classes and auditions on time. Just Momma taking care of me! Speaking of Momma taking care of me, she also told me that I should check out the hospital cafeterias because the food is nutritious and inexpensive.

Early that Sunday morning Daddy and Momma drove me to the Greyhound Bus Station downtown on Canal Street. My heart was pounding, I was so nervous and excited at the same time. When we got to the bus station, we went inside to buy my ticket. I stepped up to the ticket window and asked for a one-way ticket to New York City. Then as I reached for my wallet, my momma put her hand on my arm and said, "Leave your wallet in your pocket." My daddy stepped in and said, "This is from your momma and me," and paid for my bus ticket. That meant so much to me because I knew they couldn't really afford it, they just wanted to make sure I had some extra cash to take with me. I had managed to save about $300 working at the bank plus the $100 my parents gave me for my graduation. So I had a total of $400 in traveler's checks. Wow, I was rich! I kissed Momma and hugged Daddy as I thanked them both.

Just before I climbed aboard I went in front of the bus to look up at the destination sign over the big front window; it displayed "NEW YORK CITY." You see, I would sit on the corner of my street and Highway 90 East, heading toward Mississippi. As I sipped my Coca-Cola, I would hope that the Greyhound bus heading for New York City would pass by soon. When it did pass, I would pray that someday, when I was old enough, I would be on that bus to New York City. Now I am old enough and about to step aboard the bus to chase my dream. Then I saw my ballet teacher Gayle. How sweet of her to come to the bus station to say good-bye. I gave Gayle a hug, kissed my momma, and hugged my daddy good-bye and climbed aboard my bus.

I sat next to a window and waved good-bye. My momma was crying, and Gayle was jumping up and down with joy. My daddy had a look of sadness which I had never seen on his face before. As the bus backed out of the parking lot, I could still smell the pleasant scent of Momma's perfume. It reminded me of a time when I was probably seven years old; in our neighborhood was a Community Center and at Christmastime there was a party for the neighborhood kids. At a particular time, Santa Claus suddenly appeared. The adults put all of us kids in a line to sit on Santa's lap. We were to tell Santa if we had been good or bad and what we wanted for Christmas. It was my turn: I climbed onto Santa's lap. All of a sudden I got a whiff of what smelled like Momma's perfume, I looked Santa in the eyes, and at that very moment, I knew that I was sitting on my momma's lap! When she realized that I recognized her, she quickly whispered in my ear that if I wanted

Santa to bring me any presents for Christmas, I was not to tell my brothers about this. Knowing my momma, she was just kidding about the "no presents" thing. A few weeks later, I was snooping around in my parents' closet and found some wrapped Christmas presents. That's when I knew for sure there was no Santa Claus.

Anyway, back on the Greyhound bus: We drove up Canal Street and headed east on Highway 90. As we were getting close to my street, I noticed a young boy with a Coca-Cola sitting on the corner where I used to sit. I wondered if that boy had the same dream that I had. Maybe! I sat back in my seat, lit up a cigarette, and took a deep sigh, as my childhood faded behind me.

CHAPTER 8

New York City and Broadway

I HAD NEVER traveled further north than Macon, Georgia, so as the bus motored up the East Coast, my face was glued to the bus window. In school, we were told that the Mason-Dixon Line divided the North from the South. Early the next morning we approached the border of Maryland, heading towards Pennsylvania. I remembered that the Mason-Dixon Line was somewhere between these two states. I started looking for a sign that indicated that we were crossing the Mason-Dixon Line. Well, I never saw that sign. I just wanted to know when the bus entered into "Yankee country"! I only knew we actually crossed that line because when we stopped for breakfast, there were no grits or biscuits on the menu. Welcome to the north.

As we traveled further into Pennsylvania we passed through Philadelphia. I was reminded of a newspaper article back home. It was when I danced in *How to Succeed in Business Without Really Trying* at Gallery Circle Theatre located in the French Quarter. At one of the performances, there was a representative of The Pennsylvania Ballet Company who saw the show and afterward spoke to the director. She said that she was "struck by Dennis' dancing"—and no I didn't kick her.

TO DENNIS EDINFIELD, it felt like an ordinary Gallery Circle performance of its holdover success, "How to Succeed In Business Without Really Trying". But fate reached out from the audience. In town early for a luncheon performance next day, lecturer Judith Keith of Philadelphia attended, was struck by Dennis' dancing . . . and just happens to be the public-relations powerhouse for the Pennsylvania Ballet Co. "We want that boy for our company; he's superb," she announced to director Bob Cahlman. She'll issue a formal audition

"We want that boy for our company; he's superb," she announced to the director. She said she would issue a formal audition bid in writing. "Lucky thing," she added, "I read in the program notes that he wanted to head for New York soon. We'll just detour him our way." With only a half a dozen permanent ballet companies in the country to scramble for posts, it ranks as a major breakthrough for the young Orleanian.

After a long ride from New Orleans, the skyline of New York City finally came into sight, and a beautiful view it was! My heart was beating with anticipation. Finally, we approached the Lincoln Tunnel. I couldn't believe I was almost there and my childhood dream of performing on Broadway was just at the other end of that tunnel. At last, the bus pulled into the Port Authority bus station in New York City. I took my footlocker and hailed a cab to take me to the YMCA Sloan House on 34th Street. My friend Jack Payne suggested this YMCA because they had rooms to rent on a daily basis. Just one room, the bathrooms, and showers were down the hall, and they were communal. So I checked in and dropped off my footlocker. With my paperback book titled *New York City on $5 a Day*—yes, really $5—I took to the streets of New York. *New York City on $5 a Day* was a sightseeing guide to the city and filled with helpful information. It listed all the Broadway theatres, all the major sights to see, along with street maps categorized by neighborhoods and places to eat inexpensively. One of the restaurants was a steak house where you could get a fire-grilled steak with a baked potato, a small salad, and a big piece of Texas toast with garlic butter. All this at the cost of, wait for it, $1.75. And it was good!

The first bank I came to I opened an account and deposited some of my traveler's checks. Then I stopped for lunch at a coffee shop called Chock Full o' Nuts. I had not heard of this place, but I think it was listed in my book. I sat at the counter and ordered a hamburger and fries. When my hamburger was put on the counter in front of me, I was a little hesitant. My burger was sitting on a strange bun; burgers back home came on a big bun with sesame seeds. I asked, "What's that?" I was told it was an English muffin. What's that? I was hungry so I ate it and loved it. I'm already being introduced to new things, and I have only been on the streets of New York City for a half hour. Fun! As I was walking crosstown on 42nd Street heading east to Broadway, I just happened to look up at the side of the New Amsterdam Theatre building and noticed a faded painted sign on the side of the building that read "Ziegfeld, Glorifying The American Girl." Wow! This is the theatre where he presented The Ziegfeld Follies. How exciting! 42nd Street was different in the days of Ziegfeld—a lively street with many active theatres of music hall shows and plays. In 1966, it was in distress. There were only B-rated movies and a sprinkle of X-rated movies.

Then I made my way to the Majestic Theatre—I think it was the Majestic—where *Funny Girl* was playing. As I approached the theatre, I could see the billboard that said "*Funny Girl* starring Mimi Hines"; that stopped me in my tracks! I couldn't believe it—when did this happen? I went to the box office only to find out that Barbra Streisand had left the show. I walked away with tears in my eyes. I'd waited for a long time to see Barbra Streisand in *Funny Girl*. After the show opened on Broadway, the cast album was released. My momma was working at Sears in the music department, and as soon as it arrived in the store she bought the album for me. She knew how crazy I was for Barbra. Oh well, I still wanted to see the show, and I liked Mimi Hines. So I bought a ticket for $6.25. Yay! I was going to see *Funny Girl*. Later that night, after I had my yummy steak dinner for $1.75, I made my way to the theatre to see my first Broadway show! As I sat there in my seat listening to a full orchestra play the wonderful overture, I had goose bumps. Throughout the performance all I could think about was "I want to be up on that stage."

The next morning, at breakfast, I was introduced to bagels. Like English muffins, I had never heard of bagels. I was told that a bagel was a Jewish roll and kosher—"kosher," what's that? The waitress said to me that bagels are usually eaten with a "schmear of cream cheese." A schmear? "And better than that, add some lox." Lox, oh come on! I was born and raised in New Orleans, which is very Catholic; I don't think I even knew a Jewish person back home. Could a good Catholic boy from New Orleans eat a Jewish bagel with a smear of cream cheese and lox? Would I have to go to Confession for eating Jewish food? Whatever—I ordered the bagel with a smear of cream cheese and lox and absolutely loved it.

The next day, I made my way to Central Park. It is huge! I started on the west side and made my way across to the east side. Halfway, I spent some time at the Bethesda Fountain. It is the most photographed spot in the park. As I approached Fifth Avenue I noticed this elegant woman with her two young kids sitting on a park bench. As I got closer I realized it was Jacqueline Kennedy and the kids, Caroline and little John Jr. Not wanting to invade their privacy and knowing that the Secret Service was near, I quickly turned around and left the area. As soon as I found a phone booth I called, of course, my momma!

The next day, after a lot of sightseeing and walking , I went to the

Automat on 57th Street for lunch. I remember seeing an Automat in a movie. It was fun—all the food is behind glass windows. You pick out what you want to eat and open the window and take out the plate of food. I think that I had an egg-salad sandwich. After lunch I bought the trade papers to check out the auditions. The summer stock theatres auditioned in late March and April, so a lot was going on. Jack told me to audition only for the Equity theatres. He said that the best way for me to get my Equity card was to do summer stock at an Equity theatre. And you really needed your Equity card to work on Broadway and in most other theatres around the country. FYI, Actors Equity is the union representing professional actors and stage managers. In those days there was more Equity employment than non-Equity. In the seventies, and I'm guessing here, it all turned around. Now, there is more non-Equity work than Equity work. Obviously, this was a result of the economy and the Equity contracts' increasing demands like salaries, health insurance, and pension plans. I have directed shows in the past with a mix of Equity and non-Equity performers. Being non-Equity doesn't mean you are not as talented as the Equity actor standing next to you on stage. Some actors choose not to join Equity. They make less money, but continue to hone their craft on stage and spend less time as a cater-waiter.

I went to a couple of dance studios that Jack and Gayle suggested. I got a schedule of the classes and who was teaching them. I took ballet class at the Joffrey school and ballet from Nanette Charisse, modern jazz with Luigi, where you could see Liza Minnelli taking class, Jamie Rodgers from *West Side Story*, and Matt Maddox from *Seven Brides For Seven Brothers*—that's only a few. I took as many classes as I could afford.

My first Sunday in New York I called home, which I would do every Sunday. Momma told me that Jack wanted to get in touch with me about an audition. So as soon as I said good-bye to the family, I called

Jack. He told me that his good friend Carl Jablonski was assisting the choreographer, Ernie Flatt, on the new Broadway show *Superman*. He gave me Carl's phone number and said I should call, because it turns out that one of the dancers in *Superman* might be leaving the show soon and his replacement would have to dance and be able to tumble. Now I was nervous. I didn't expect my first audition to be for a Broadway show. The next morning I went to the Alvin Theatre, now the Neil Simon Theatre. Carl met me in the lobby and took me downstairs to the lower lobby and introduced me to Mr. Flatt. I wanted to say, "Do you remember me from the convention in New Orleans?" but I was afraid he might say "No." He explained that the dancer that I might replace hadn't officially given his notice and there was a chance that he might not. I don't remember much of the audition except that they were both very kind to me. I was glad when it was over and very glad that they didn't say that I should get on the bus and go back home to New Orleans. I guess the dancer did not leave the show after all because I never heard from them. That was alright because a few years later I would be dancing for Mr. Flatt, only in Hollywood on *The Carol Burnett Show*, and I would call him Ernie. The first time I was on Carol's show I was happy to see I would be dancing with Carl Jablonski, who is now a friend.

Later the next week, I called a friend with whom I had done a couple of shows in New Orleans. Mousey (his nickname) had moved to New York a few years before me. He invited me over to meet a couple of other people from New Orleans. A friend of mine, John, who was from my high school, was there. He and I did *How to Succeed* together in New Orleans. As it turned out John and a friend of his invited me to share a hotel suite that they were renting by the week. When you split the rent between three people, it was cheaper than staying at the Y. So I jumped at the offer. The hotel was a small four-story building, very modest. Our suite was a one-bedroom with twin beds, and in the living room there was a sofa bed. Perfect for three people.

The audition season had begun. Sometimes you could do a couple of auditions a day. The audition process was pretty much the same for all chorus calls. You were given an index card to put down your name, phone number, and address. The choreographer would use the back of the card to grade your dancing. You were put into groups of ten or more depending on how many people showed up to audition. Sometimes it was close to one hundred. Everyone would learn a dance routine, usually a jazz and ballet combination. Then they would call us out on stage group by group. After you danced you were told to go to the stage left wing or stage right wing. One wing was for the dancers who would be staying for the next round, and the other wing was for those who would be going home. Then the next group would dance and so on. I learned very quickly that if I felt I was in the wing with the not-so-good dancers, I would step forward and raise my hand and say to the choreographer, "I can tumble too." At that time there were very few dancers who also tumbled. They would ask me to do some tumbling, and I did, and they would say, "You can stay." One day as I was checking out the trade paper I saw an audition notice for Starlight Musicals. Starlight Musicals was in Indianapolis and a very sought-after job. They were known for using stars in the lead roles.

So off I go to the auditions for Starlight. When I walked into the audition room I noticed a familiar face—it was Bob Audy. Mr. Audy taught at the National Dance Convention I'd attended back home. He was choreographing the season at Starlight. I think when he saw me walk into the studio, he remembered me. I nailed the audition. I danced my best ever, and I sang "You Are Sixteen Going On Seventeen" beautifully. At the end of the audition, I was hired for the summer. I was so excited and proud. I was going to get my Equity card. The first thing I did after the audition was to call Momma. She was thrilled! A few days later my Equity contract arrived at the hotel. So I got dressed up to sign it, just in case I became famous and wrote a book someday.

Then I went to the Equity office to file my contract, make a deposit on my dues, and pick up my Equity card.

**With the stroke of a pen, I became a professional actor.
Momma sent the tape recorder on the desk along with
some of my tapes of several Broadway musicals.**

I continued going to class and auditioning, just for the experience. I wanted to get my face out there and dance and sing for as many directors and choreographers as possible. I did receive a couple of offers from other summer stock theatres I auditioned for. It felt great to say, "Thank you for the offer, but I just signed a contract, so my summer

is booked." I was feeling very confident that I had made the right decision to move to New York City and pursue a career.

My job at Starlight Musicals wasn't going to start until the end of
June, and while I was in New York, I wanted to see all the shows that I
could afford. I got to see *Mame* with Angela Lansbury. She and the music and the choreography were incredible. A few years later I will have
the privilege of doing a movie with Angela Lansbury. I also got to see
Sweet Charity, starring the stunning Gwen Verdon and directed/cho-
reographed by Gwen Verdon's husband, Bob Fosse. This fantastic show
performed at the famous Palace Theatre. There's an old saying in show
business: "You haven't made it until you've played the Palace." I will
never forget the moment when the conductor raised his baton, and the
brass in the orchestra played the first six chords of "Big Spender"—I
was on the ceiling. To be sitting in the Palace Theatre on Broadway and
enjoying this brand-new musical made me feel like I had come home.

At the beginning of May, I decided to take a plane—not a bus, but a
plane—back to New Orleans to see my family and show off my Equity
card and brag about my first professional job. One night I was hanging
out with some theatre friends in the Quarter when it was suggested
that we have a beer before I took the bus home. We went to Dixie's.
Dixie's was the first "gay" bar in the French Quarter and just steps from
Pat O'Brien's. It would not be my first time in a gay bar.

After a beer I decided it was time to catch the bus. As I started to
leave I saw my Aunt Dede sitting with a friend at the bar; she must be
on her break from Pat's. Oh my God, I felt trapped. I didn't want Aunt
Dede to see me in this gay bar—she might just mention to Momma
that she saw me at Dixie's. So I just had to walk past her and hope she
didn't see me. Well, she did see me. So I stopped to say hello with a
quick kiss on the cheek and explained that I was running to catch the
next bus home. My only hope now was that she wouldn't remember
seeing me. The next day Momma approached me with tears in her

eyes. She had been hanging up my pants when a matchbook fell out of my pocket onto the floor. When she picked it up she saw that it was from Dixie's Bar. She asked me if I had been in Dixie's and was I like them, "queer." It was the way she said "queer" that felt like a knife in my heart. The label "gay" was not used yet. I knew in a heartbeat that this was not the time to "come out" to my momma. She would never understand, so I lied. It just killed me that I couldn't tell my momma the truth about who I was; in fact at that time I didn't quite understand myself why I was like I was, gay. It was 1966, and nobody was out. It was against the law to be homosexual, and it was considered a mental illness. So, I just had to lie. I answered, "No, Momma, I'm not." The subject was never brought up again.

CHAPTER 9

Summer Stock

THE SUMMER SEASON of '66 at The Starlight Musicals included *Kiss Me Kate* starring Patrice Munsell, a Metropolitan Opera star; *Gentlemen Prefer Blondes* starring Carroll Baker, beautiful star of *Baby Doll* and *Harlow*; *The Jack Benny Show* with his guest Wayne Newton; *Music Man* with Forrest Tucker, star of TV show *F Troop*; *Oklahoma*, starring Gordon MacRae, famous singing movie star; and *How To Succeed In Business*, starring Van Johnson, famous MGM movie star.

The schedule was exhausting. We rehearsed one week for each show. After the first show opened, we started rehearsing during the day for the next show coming up. We rehearsed one show during the day and performed the other show in the evening. No day off. We did have a little break with the schedule (since we were not in the Jack Benny Show, we had the evenings off while he did his show), but we still rehearsed during the day for the next show. Doing summer stock is hard work. When I started directing I would begin the first day of rehearsals with, "This is summer stock, not summer camp, so be prepared to work." Yes, summer stock was hard work, but I would return to New York with a lot of experience and five professional shows on my resume.

On my birthday there was a party for me, and at the time we were rehearsing *Gentlemen Prefer Blondes* starring Carroll Baker. I was in a scene with her that we rehearsed earlier in the day. She was sweet to show up so she could wish the birthday boy a "Happy Birthday." When she knocked on the door I opened it, and she remembered me from rehearsal and asked me if I could point out the birthday boy. I told her she was looking at the birthday boy. She smiled, wished me a "Happy Birthday," and gave me a hug and a kiss on the cheek.

Momma, along with Grandma Kelly and my Aunt Connie, decided to drive up to Indianapolis to see me perform in the last performance of *Oklahoma*. After the show, they showered me with praise. I took them backstage where they got to meet Gordon MacRae and have their picture taken with him. They were thrilled! The next evening they went to the opening night of *How to Succeed in Business Without Really Trying* starring Van Johnson.

After the show I brought them to the opening-night party. It was being thrown by one of the socialites who was on the Board of Directors of the theatre. Her home was a large mansion with a pool on the back lawn. I introduced my family to everyone in the cast along with the producer, director, choreographer, and hostess. Momma had a wonderful time, and she fit in like she was one of us. After about an hour Momma said that they were leaving because they wanted to get an early start back to New Orleans the next morning. That's when I told her that at the end of the summer I was going back to New York to find an apartment and pursue my career. She said she had a feeling that I would and said she was proud of me and she was so happy I was following my dream. When she kissed me good night, she said, "I guess I will always be saying good-bye to you, Dennis; I love you and take care of yourself and don't forget to call home on Sundays." This would be the last time that I would see my momma. The next day on a two-lane highway somewhere in the state of Tennessee, a driver pulled out from behind a truck and ran head-on into their car, killing Momma and Grandma Kelly. My aunt was badly injured and survived.

I did not find out about the accident until after the show when I was called into the producer's office. The couple who'd hosted Aunt Connie, Momma, and Grandma were there. I thought they had seen the show and wanted to compliment me. No, they were there to tell me that Aunt Connie called to say that there was a car accident and Momma and Grandma were killed. I couldn't believe what I was hearing. I went into shock. Then the producer handed me the phone. I took the phone and my Aunt Dorothy, my momma's sister, said "Dennis." I thought it was Momma. She sounded like Momma. I said, "Momma, they told me that you were dead," to which she said, "It's your Aunt Dorothy, Dennis. I'm sorry to say your momma is dead." That's when I lost it. The next thing I knew I was on a plane for New Orleans.

When I got home, I walked into our house to find a bunch of relatives there. After I said hello to everyone, one of my aunts said that my daddy was lying down in the bedroom, but he wanted to know when I got home. So I went into my parents' bedroom and found that Daddy had cried himself to sleep. I then went to the other bedroom where my two brothers were lying down. When I walked in, my little brother Randy sat up in bed. I had never seen his young 15-year-old face looking so sad, and Timmy looked like he was in shock. Later my daddy got up, and the aunts and uncles tried to comfort us with food. Eventually, the relatives went to the motel where they were staying. Now it was just Daddy and my brothers and me. As we sat there in the living room, not really speaking, I still couldn't believe that Momma was never coming home, and now it was just the four of us. Momma was the matriarch, and now nothing would be the same with our family. This left me feeling lonely. I had this hole in my heart. After they went to bed, I fell asleep on the couch.

Later in the morning my Aunt Dorothy came to our home and told me that my daddy wasn't really strong enough to go with her to pick out a coffin, and she would like me to go with her.

We went to the funeral home and found a nice coffin, and later we picked the prettiest dress for Momma to be laid out in; it was a dress that Momma had made for herself. The wake was very painful for everyone, because everybody loved my momma. The next day was the funeral, and afterwards a lot of the family went to the West End to "Fitzgerald's Seafood Restaurant". That's what the Kellys do after a funeral. Later my daddy told me that Momma would want me to go back to work and finish the season. The next day I flew back to Indianapolis and rejoined the cast. At the end of the season, I went back to New York City as planned.

CHAPTER 10

My First Apartment

BACK IN NEW York, I shared an apartment with another actor from Starlight Musicals. The small apartment was a five-flight walk-up on West 81ˢᵗ Street just off Columbus Avenue. In 1966 this was not a good neighborhood but was affordable. Today it's an expensive neighborhood.

I started auditioning and went back to my dance and singing classes. I enrolled in acting classes at the HB Studios. I auditioned for a new Broadway show, *Breakfast At Tiffany's* starring Mary Tyler Moore. I didn't get the job. Michael Kidd, the famous choreographer, told me I looked too young to go to a Holly Golightly party. However, I had tumbled for him at the audition, and he told me to please audition for him again. He loved dancers who could tumble. I also auditioned for a musical titled *A Joyful Noise,* choreographed by a young Michael Bennett; I didn't get that job either. However, later in my life, Michael would have a significant influence on my career.

Director/choreographer Gower Champion was holding auditions for two male dancers as replacements in the national tour of *Hello Dolly*, starring Betty Grable. On the day of the audition, I showed up at the stage door of the St. James Theatre and signed in. I didn't count all the names above mine, but there must have been close to a hundred guys auditioning for just two spots. It was thrilling to audition for the very successful Gower Champion, and on the stage of the St. James Theatre, where the biggest hit show on Broadway, *Hello Dolly*, was playing. As usual, we were divided up into groups and taught a dance combination from the show. It was from the musical number "Dancing," so it was somewhat balletic. After the first go-round of cuts, meaning dancers being let go, we learned another combination and another round of cuts. Finally, we were lined up across the stage, and two people were called out of line: Sal Pernice and myself. The rest were told, "Thank you for coming, you may leave." Then Gower said that he would like both of us to join the national tour. He told Sal that he would be in the chorus and understudy the role of Barnaby. Then Gower offered me the "swing dancer" spot. Now, I didn't know what that was—a swing dancer? I was so excited to have the job, I didn't ask. Well, I would soon find out. I think it was a week later that Michael Bennett called to offer me a job touring in a production of *West Side Story* that he was directing and choreographing. Of course, I had to say no because I was leaving the next day to join the *Hello Dolly* company in Chicago.

The day I arrived in Chicago, I checked into the hotel where the other cast members were staying. Later I went to the Shubert Theatre to report to the stage manager. I walked in the stage door and signed in on the cast list. As I was signing in, I heard someone coming down the spiral staircase. As I looked up, the first thing I saw were those gorgeous legs. I knew they had to belong to Betty Grable.

The *"Hello Dolly"* Production Number
I'm second on Betty's left.

"Put On Your Sunday Clothes"
I'm on the train standing next to the letter 'S' in the YONKERS sign.

The Waiters' Gallop
I'm third from the left.

Betty always wore a man's white dress shirt to have her makeup applied. As she continued down the stairs, I was reminded that her legs were insured for one million dollars by Lloyd's of London. Her legs were beautiful, perfect. I stayed and watched the show that night, and Miss Grable was wonderful along with the entire cast—some I recognized from when I saw the show in New Orleans. I was filled with pride as I realized that I was now a member of this wonderful cast and the biggest Broadway hit!

The next day was my first day of rehearsal. I went to the theatre and met the dance captain, Jack Craig, who was going to teach me the show. Now I was about to find out what being a swing really means - and it terrified me! He explained to me that my job was to cover (understudy) the twelve dancers and five singers in the show. This feeling of panic swept over me. At this stage of my career, I was not experienced enough to cover seventeen people, all with different tracks. Thank God Jack Craig sensed I was a little inexperienced and not ready to understudy twelve dancers and five singers, so he taught me his tracks first. "Tracks" are like a map showing when and where the dancer moves next. So when someone was out of the show, I would go on for Jack and he would cover for the person who was out of the show. Eventually, I did learn all of the tracks, but I still would have to rely on my notes which I kept in the wings. When I had to go on for someone, my show was all about "where do I go next and when." The choreography was complicated because the male dancers all had different tracks. It was very stressful, and I was still grieving my momma's death. I was not in a good place, emotionally. It was a couple of months before I felt like I had a good performance.

Me and Betty on the road with *Hello Dolly*

I really liked Betty. She was charming and a wonderful Dolly. And I knew she liked me. Except, there was this one time when I was on for someone who was out of the show. In the "Dolly" number, Dolly sings, "Hello Manny well hello Danny," and I was supposed to step forward when she sang "Hello Danny" and nod to her. I didn't because I didn't remember that I was Danny. This was not a good thing. My mistake left her standing there. After the show she summoned me to her dressing room to let me know she was not happy. I apologized and promised that it wouldn't happen again. And it didn't. Sometimes Betty would invite some of us to her hotel suite after the show to watch reels of her movies. She would order pizzas and tell us "behind-the-scene stories" about making this movie and what crazy thing happened on that movie. It was fun! There were other times a bunch of us would go to this piano bar where we would sing a song or two, usually our audition songs. This was before karaoke. I toured with the show for several months until we closed. It was very sad to watch the load in of the show for the last time; oh well, back to New York I go to find another job.

When I got back to the city, I auditioned for a revival of *Finian's Rainbow* at The New York City Center starring Nancy Dussault and Frank McHugh. Also in the cast was newcomer Sandy Duncan. At the audition, the choreographer taught the dancers a routine and then we were asked to sing "Happy Birthday." The singers got to sing their audition song, but the dancers could only sing "Happy Birthday," as if dancers couldn't sing, and on that note, dancers never got to say lines in the play, as if we couldn't talk either. Those went to the singers. I heard on TV that morning that it was Bette Davis's birthday. So I sang "Happy Birthday, Bette Davis," and everybody laughed. I got the job—it was my first Broadway credit. All the shows at City Center were limited runs, so I was still out there auditioning for the next job.

After *Finian's* closed, I received a phone call from the David Merrick office. David Merrick was the producer of *Hello Dolly*. Betty Grable was coming to Broadway to do *Dolly*, and they wanted me to join the cast. Wow, another Broadway show. Then I heard the words "swing dancer." My heart sank. I just could not do that to myself again, swing 17 performers, and I knew I had probably forgotten most of the tracks in the show. All of a sudden I heard myself say, "No." I couldn't believe I was turning down *Hello Dolly* on Broadway, but I did. I explained that if another spot opened up in the show that was not the swing dancer, I would be thrilled to join the cast. I said "thank you for the offer" and the call ended. I was so disappointed, I'm sure I must have cried. Today, Equity requires more than one swing for both the male and female ensembles, which is how it should have been back then.

A few weeks later, I was cast in *Hellzapoppin*. The show was going to preview at the World's Fair, also known as Expo 67, in Montreal, Canada, and then the show would move to Broadway. Well, I still had *Hellzapoppin*. *Hellzapoppin* was a vaudeville show starring Soupy Sales, who was perfect for this show. There were several supporting players. There was this sketch where one of the actresses, a very funny comedian, walks into the audience with another actor in a gorilla costume. By the way, the theatre was in the round and more like a nightclub setting. Soupy says to the lady with the gorilla, "You can't bring a gorilla in here, where is he going to sit?" She says, "Anywhere he wants to," at which time the gorilla comes up to me. I am seated like an audience member. He then picks me up by the collar of my coat, leads me to a staircase, makes a scary gorilla sound at me, and I do a backflip down the stairs out of sight.

The Expo was located on three islands. The theatre where we played was Le Jardin on the island La Ronde. Quebec is a French province. They spoke some English. I studied French in high school for one semester because I was studying ballet. After the show one night we went to a very nice restaurant for fondue. After dinner, I said to the waitress, "L'addition, s'il vous plaît," and she looked at me and said, "You mean the check?" Not giving up I said, "wee," and she pointed in the direction of the bathroom. I was so confused.

I celebrated my twenty-first birthday while in Montreal. Soupy had a fun party for me and the whole cast was there. I really liked Soupy and the cast. We had a fun time performing the show. On a not-so-"fun" note, one night in the sketch with the gorilla, as I did the backflip my heel caught the back of the step and down the stairs I went. I badly injured my knee. I was taken to the hospital and the X-ray showed that I needed surgery. The next day I was on a plane back to New York City. While I was in New York recovering from surgery, *Hellzapoppin* closed and would not make it back to Broadway.

CHAPTER 11

Recovery and Return to Work

THE SURGERY WAS a success, and I underwent many weeks of physical therapy and weeks on crutches. My surgery was before the arthroscopic surgery was available, so my healing took longer. My doctor finally gave me the OK to go back to dance class. Now the question was, can I still tumble? I needed to find out. Although my reputation as a triple threat (actor/dancer/singer) was well-established at this stage of my career, the tumbling was a big extra. The more you bring to the table, the better your chances of being hired. I walked over to Central Park and found a good grassy area. I stood for a long time in preparation to do a back somersault. My brain couldn't connect to the muscle memory of how to do a back somersault. A lot of the delay was definitely fear that I might damage my knee again. When it comes to tumbling, the worst thing is fear. What if I can't ever do a back somersault ever again? Then all of a sudden I went for it and landed on my feet. I did it! It was a little painful, but, I did it. As a dancer, you get used to a little pain. We dancers know the expression, "If it doesn't hurt, you're not doing it right." As I was walking back home, I felt great relief.

In the spring of 1968, I was back dancing again. I was hired to dance on the Kraft Music Hall. This was a summer show with a new host every week.

This particular show was hosted by John Davidson with guests Michele Lee, Tom Jones, The Fifth Dimension, Lou Rawls, Buffy Sainte-Marie, and Prof. Irwin Cory. If I forgot someone, please forgive me. This was when I met a dancer who would have a positive influence on my life and career, Roy Smith. It turned out that Roy knew my mentor, Jack Payne. They were both from Texas. Over the years we would do many of the same television shows and movies. Roy and I would become the best of friends, like brothers.

Next, I was cast in a production of *Kiss Me Kate* with Patrice Munsel and John Cullum. This was the second time that I did *Kiss Me Kate* with Patrice. In one of the scenes, there was a need for a donkey. You see, Petruchio had to put Kate across the donkey's back in a scene following their wedding. One of the dancers, Gene, who was smaller, was cast as the front of the donkey, and I got to be the back part of the donkey where Kate would ride. Gene and I got to be good friends. I guess when you spend months bent over in half with your nose almost up somebody's butt, sorta, you get kind of close. We were also cast as Petruchio's slaves.

The show played a theatre in Mineola, New York, way out on Long Island. This was to keep the New York critics away because there was hope for a Broadway Revival with this production. And this production was great! Along with Patrice and John, the cast was rounded out with Broadway talent.

Finally, the Broadway Revival was a go except there was no Broadway theatre available. To keep the cast and show together the producers took the show to Canada. We toured for a while, and still, no Broadway theatre was available. Eventually, our contracts ran out, and the producers couldn't afford to keep the show in Canada any longer, so we closed out-of-town and went home. Not counting *Hello Dolly*, which I'd turned down, this was my second loss of a possible Broadway show. I was quickly learning that show business can be full of disappointments.

CHAPTER 12

1968: Off to Hollywood

AFTER THE DISAPPOINTMENT of *Kiss Me Kate* not going to Broadway, I decided I was going to move to Hollywood and be an actor. No more chorus boy for me. I bought a convertible in New Jersey—you have to have a convertible in Hollywood—and started to pack. I gave up my garden apartment to a friend, Sammy Williams, who would go on to win a Tony Award in 1975 as Best Actor in a Musical. Gene also decided to give it a try in Hollywood. So we were off to LaLa Land.

On our way to Hollywood, we stopped in Tampa, Florida, to do two shows at The Tampa Summer Musicals. I was assisting the choreographer, and at the auditions in New York, we hired a great cast, including a friend of Gene's he'd studied ballet with, Sachi Shimizu, and another dancer named Vicki Fredricks. Both of them were extremely talented performers and would do *A Chorus Line* later in their careers.

After the Tampa gig ended, we left for Hollywood. As we drove across the country, we stopped in the panhandle of Florida to visit my daddy, who had moved back to the Edenfield farm. Then we visited New Orleans for a few days. Eventually, we were driving over the San Gabriel Mountains. I will never forget seeing the Pacific Ocean for the first time. It was magnificently breathtaking. When we arrived in Hollywood, we stopped for breakfast. I bought the trade paper *Variety* and read that there was going to be an audition that morning for *The Red Skelton Show*. I used to watch this show with my family, and I loved the dancers. Although I'd moved to Hollywood to be an actor— "no more chorus boy for me"—I needed a job. So off to CBS Television City to audition.

Hollywood was very different from New York City—sunshine, palm trees, and clean air—at least it was back then. It was early August, and the weather was perfect. When we drove up to the guard at CBS Television City, he gave instructions on where to go for the audition. Walking into this very large studio, I couldn't believe how many people were there to audition. As I made my way through the crowd, I spotted my good friend from New York City, Roy Smith. Roy was in *Mame* on Broadway when we first met. Miss Lansbury had a big holiday party, and Roy invited me to go with him. It was wonderful. She lived in this exquisite penthouse on the east side of Manhattan. There were lots of celebrities at this elegant party.

Roy had been in Hollywood for a couple of weeks, so while we were waiting to dance he filled me in on what was happening work-wise. I filled out my dance card with my info. Since I had just arrived in town, I didn't have a phone number. No cell phones back then. I did give the number of my answering service in New York City. Finally, the audition started. The choreographer, Tom Hansen, welcomed us and explained that he needed only one male and one female dancer. He and his assistant then put us into groups according to the number on our cards. Then we began to learn a dance routine. Unfortunately, Gene twisted his ankle and had to drop out of the audition. He would eventually go back to New York and dance in a couple of Broadway shows and, with his partner, open a very successful dance studio.

The eliminations went on and on until there were only a few

dancers left including myself and Roy. I considered raising my hand and saying "I can tumble," but I didn't. I was a bit conflicted because I came to Hollywood to get out of the chorus. We stood there in a line while Tom and his assistant, Brenda, looked us over and whispered stuff about us and finally all that was said was "Thank you all for coming." That's it. We picked up our dance bags and left the studio.

Then a couple of days later I went to audition for *The Hollywood Palace*. The Hollywood Palace was just off Hollywood Boulevard and Vine. My friend Roy was there and told me that Tom Hansen was trying to get in touch with me and I should call him at CBS. I immediately went to a phone booth and called CBS. I was put in touch with someone in the Skelton office, and eventually I was offered the job on *The Red Skelton Show*, now called *The Red Skelton Comedy Hour*. Oh my God, I was going to dance with some of the best dancers on television. I'm going to be a Tom Hansen Dancer—what an honor! And thank you, Roy Smith—what a friend.

One of the great things about being on the Skelton show was, we danced a lot more than the dancers on some of the other shows. We did an opening number to David Rose's "Holiday for Strings" and ended the show with the same number. We did a number with the musical guest stars of the week, and then we got to have our own production number, starring The Tom Hansen Dancers.

The first day of work I walked into the large studio and saw the dancers whom I recognized from television sitting around a table. Yes, we had our own table? In New York, we only had a chair. Plus, I think, I remember another table with donuts and bagels and cream cheese. Pretty much all the TV shows and movies used Craft Services, an industry catering company that provided food and drinks throughout the entire rehearsal and shooting process. Speaking of industry, in Hollywood, film and television was referred to as "the Industry." In New York City, it's all referred to as "the Business," as in show business.

Tom Hansen was working on a routine, and Brenda, his assistant, was writing song lyrics on a moveable blackboard. Eventually, we were called onto the dance floor, and Tom explained the production number to us, and then we learned the choreography. As we danced, we sang the lyrics that were on the blackboard. We taped all the musical numbers on Wednesday morning and afternoon with no audience, which meant if someone dropped a hat or messed up a step, Tom could stop the tape and fix it. So, the final result and what you saw on TV was a perfect musical dance number. Mr. Skelton taped his show in front of a live audience on a Tuesday.

The season was about 23 weeks. In the fall we taped 13 shows, and then we went on hiatus for several weeks and then we returned after the holidays to finish the remaining 13 weeks. These numbers may be off—I mean it was a long time ago. Every week there was a new musical guest star or two. During rehearsals they would sit with us and socialize. I remember Merv Griffin guest-starring on the Skelton show. One day at rehearsal Merv told a funny story. He had been the rehearsal pianist for *The Kate Smith Show*—I think that's correct. She was known for her hit song "When the Moon Comes Over the Mountain," and that was her theme music for her show. Miss Smith would introduce her guest by singing, "And this week we have (guest's name)," all to the tune of "When the Moon Comes Over the Mountain." When they were rehearsing the introduction of her guest star Tallulah Bankhead, Miss Bankhead was late with her entrance. Miss Smith was overheard saying, "Is she going to make that entrance on time?" as Miss Bankhead enters behind her and replies, "I will be making entrances while you are still trying to pull that damn moon over the mountain." Another funny story was from Dale Evans when she and Roy Rogers were guests on the Skelton show. She told us that she bought Roy a new pair of shoes. Roy preferred his cowboy boots. Somehow the shoes went missing, and Roy told Dale he had left them on the porch and that he thought a big wildcat had gotten them and carried the shoes off into the hills. A couple of days later Roy Rogers pulled up to the porch with a dead wildcat over Trigger's back. When Dale saw this, she sang, "Is that the cat that chewed your new shoes?" to the tune of "Is that the Chattanooga Choo?" It was funny. I guess you had to be there.

I continued to do a lot of television in Hollywood. I danced many times on *The Carol Burnett Show*. I enjoyed working with Carol. She was friendly and wonderful to be around. She and Harvey, Tim, Vicki, and Lyle really made everyone laugh. Back then there were many musical variety shows on TV. This meant a lot of work for dancers and singers in Hollywood. At CBS there was *The Red Skelton Show*, *The Carol Burnett Show*, *Sonny and Cher*, Smothers Brothers and Jim Nabors, just to name a few. I casually knew these terrific people. I mean you ride in the elevators with them and pass them in the halls and maybe have a brief conversation. We were all part of the CBS Television City Family. Don't misunderstand me—it's not like we hung out together.

When the weekly variety shows went on hiatus, or vacation, several TV stars would do their TV specials; I performed on many of them. Besides doing all this television, I was lucky enough to land a few films. The first film was a full-length movie of a popular kids' television show *Pufnstuf*. It was exciting to join The Screen Actors Guild. Working on a SAG contract is where you make the most money. Whether it's a film or a commercial, you know eventually you will receive residuals in the mail. The movie was shot at Universal Studios, which is, I believe, the largest film studio. It was over the Hollywood Hills into the San Fernando Valley in Studio City. I will never forget the first morning I drove over the Hollywood Hills to go to the studio. The sun was just peeking over the mountains and illuminating the valley in front of me. Exciting! The dancers, both men and women, were costumed as witches. I don't remember being told that we would be in drag. Anyway, I got my SAG card, my health insurance, and for several weeks had a good time and made lots of money. There was more money to be made in Hollywood than on Broadway. At least at that time. We had to show up in the makeup building at 7 a.m. There was a lot of makeup and appliances to be applied to turn our pretty faces into the ugly witches that we ended up being. The leads were Martha Raye, Billie Hayes, Cass Elliot (Momma Cass), and Jack Wild to name a few. There was this one time we had about an hour off before we would be needed again. One of us asked Bud Westmore, head of makeup, if we could borrow his golf cart to check out the back lot. We were gone for about 30 minutes when we were stopped by the studio police in front of the house from the movie *Psycho*. We thought that we were in some kind of trouble, but we weren't. Bud Westmore needed his cart—ASAP. So the studio police escorted us witches back to the studio. It was fun having lunch in the studio commissary where you could spot a star or two. The best food of all the studio commissaries was at the Disney Studios in Burbank. That's where I would work next.

I did *Bednobs and Broomsticks* with Angela Lansbury at the Walt Disney Studios. We did this big production number with her called *The Portabella Road*. I played an Australian soldier. My friend Roy Smith was also in this movie, and we would continue to do many of the same jobs.

In Hollywood, once you were established, you didn't have to always audition. The director or choreographer would call you or your agent and offer you the job. I liked that. I liked many things about living in Hollywood, like the weather. I enjoyed driving around in my convertible in the beautiful sunny weather. I also liked the living conditions compared to New York. In Southern California you could rent an apartment or a house for almost half of what you would pay in New York.

Also, the homes in Hollywood were newer back then. In New York it seemed like most buildings were old. The cool thing about living in a Hollywood apartment complex was, most had a swimming pool in the middle of the courtyard. One morning, after my swim, I was sitting at the dining table having my first cup of coffee when my agent, Joseph, called. Thank God, because a day that your agent doesn't call is a day of rejection. In other words, nobody wants to hire you today. Anyway, Joseph was calling about a movie offer he had received for me. I asked what was the movie about and he replied, "Sit down." Then Joseph began by explaining that this is a SAG movie titled *Chatterbox*. It was about a woman who discovers that her vagina could talk and sing. Joseph quickly added that this was not a porn movie. There was no nudity except for a brief breast shot. I said, "No nudity. What about the vagina?" and Joseph said, "It wears a costume." I did a spit take with my coffee. I did accept the job. After all, they were paying over scale and I was featured in a production number titled "Cocka Doodle Do." I was dressed as the rooster. It was a fun number. There were several known actors in this film like Larry Gelman, Candace Ralston, Jane Kean, and Rip Taylor. The movie became and still is a popular cult movie.

One late afternoon during happy hour I was at a popular restaurant in Hollywood frequented by the "industry" crowd. I was having a drink with friends at the bar when one of my new agents who I was freelancing with was there having dinner. On his way out he told me that it was not a good idea for me to be seen at this bar. When I asked why, he replied that it was known to be a gay pickup bar and he said something like—and this is not a direct quote—"I'm representing you as a young romantic leading man. Romantic with women, not men." He left the restaurant, but I didn't. I was beginning to understand that maybe there is a lot of sacrificing in return for celebrity, including your personal privacy.

I'm glad I didn't leave the restaurant that night because I met an actor named Dennis Cooney. He was a successful actor from Broadway. He was in Hollywood appearing in the hit play *The Boys in the Band*.

We became more than close friends and briefly shared an apartment in Hollywood and later in New York. After a few years, our relationship changed to just friends. We would be friends for 45 years until he passed away. He introduced me to my first agent in New York, Marge Fields. She was a successful agent who would represent me for theatre and commercials. Soon a new agent joined the agency named Dorothy Scott, and she represented me for several years. My first commercial that I booked was for J.C. Penny's Back-to-School Fashions. No tumbling or dancing. Then I did a commercial for a Whirlpool Stackable Washer/Dryer. I did tumble in this commercial. I was cast as a family member in a circus act. I tumbled from the circus tent to our trailer. Once inside the trailer, the mom of the act collected our leotards and put them in the piggyback washer and dryer, showing that you didn't need a lot of space for this new type of washer/dryer.

Finally, I was hired to play a role in a play, not a musical. It was an Off-Broadway play titled *The Evil That Men Do*. *Hair* opened on Broadway in 1968. It was a big hit—still is all over the world. In fact, *Hair* pretty much led the way for many shows to bare it all on stage. *The Evil That Men Do* had some, very brief, nudity. I didn't care about the nudity. I was proud of my body and not shy when on stage; off stage is a different story. I did the play because I wanted to be an actor, not a chorus boy. Shortly after we started previews, Equity called a strike, and the play closed before it opened.

CHAPTER 13

Bucks County Playhouse

IN THE FALL of 1970, I was doing a new musical called *Zing*. It was written by the same creators of the hit show *Dames At Sea*, which introduced Bernadette Peters to the world. The production of *Zing* was presented at the famous Bucks County Playhouse in New Hope, Pennsylvania. It was to be an out-of-town tryout before *Zing* would move to Broadway. Unfortunately, the move to Broadway never happened. However, I was asked to join the repertory company at the playhouse. We performed *West Side Story* and *Romeo and Juliet* in repertory. The day finally came that I got to be in *West Side Story*. Wow, I was blown away. This was a dream come true for me. I was cast as Bernardo. Understand I was a young 24-year-old with lots of dark wavy hair, which I combed back with a puff up front. I also had a tan and makeup helped. My accent wasn't great, but I got by.

This is *Zing* at Bucks County Playhouse. I'm on the right in both pictures.

Me as Bernardo

Patty Carr as Anita, Terry Eno
is Riff, Don McCan is Tony.
Standing is Marcia King as Maria
and me as Bernardo

New Hope is a picturesque small town with a picture-perfect village spread along the beautiful Delaware River. The village is right out of the movies and has many fine boutiques, restaurants, and antique shops. We started rehearsals in the late fall of 1970 beginning with *West Side Story* and adding *Romeo and Juliet*. The cast was housed at the inn next to the playhouse. My room was facing the Delaware River very close to the spot where George Washington made his famous crossing. It was fall, and the hills across the river were ablaze with color. I loved working at the playhouse. It was originally a gristmill. In 1939, it was transformed into a theatre. So many stars have worked at the playhouse. Stars like Helen Hayes, Lillian Gish, Grace Kelly, Tyne Daly, George C. Scott, Angela Lansbury, Robert Redford, Kim Hunter, to name a very few, graced the stage of the playhouse. *Barefoot in the Park* with Robert Redford played the playhouse before it moved to Broadway. I will always feel blessed to have joined the roster of those who had the pleasure of playing The Bucks County Playhouse. Unfortunately, I injured my left knee, again, in *West Side Story*. More surgery was needed. Again I was laid up for some time.

Me as Bernardo

Patty Carr as Anita, Terry Eno
is Riff, Don McCan is Tony. Standing is
Marcia King as Maria and me as
Bernardo

When I was able to work again, I did a couple of small roles on some soaps. I had a nice role on *The Guiding Light*. I played the character Jojo, a mechanic whose garage had burned down. There was this fantasy scene where Kim Zimmerman and I danced together, like Fred Astaire and Ginger Rogers. After our dance, it was back to reality and a scene where a friend of Kim's character offered to rebuild Jojo's garage. I also did some work on *The Secret Storm* and *Ryan's Hope*. I was still booking commercials. I booked a Vita Herring commercial. I was cast as a boxer in the ring. The storyboard—a placard on an easel showing different shots of the commercial's storyline—showed that the boxer would taste the product. Now I had never tasted herring, but I knew I didn't like it. As luck would have it, I didn't have to eat it because of the boxing gloves.

Since I was not a signed client with Marge Fields, I was able to freelance with other agencies. I did freelance with Anne Wright. The agent I worked with was Flo, who booked me on several commercials. She was great! Throughout the seventies I was a dancing cowboy in a sugar-free Dr. Pepper commercial. There was a commercial for Ace Hardware with Mary Ann Mobley, a former Miss America in 1958. I do remember watching that pageant on TV, and I even remember the question she was asked in the finals before the voting began. The question was, "If you were wearing high heels in the swimsuit competition and one of the heels broke, what would you do?" Her answer was that she never wears high heels with a bathing suit so she would just take the shoes off. When I shared this with her during a break she said she was touched that I would remember.

After that, I did a dancing Goodyear Tire commercial. Then a Ritz cracker commercial with Andy Griffith, who was very nice. The only downside with this commercial shoot was the food stylist bought only Jack cheese to dress the Ritz cracker. Jack cheese is very spicy. It looked good but after many takes of the scene where we had to eat the Ritz, our mouths were burning. Even though we were given a "spit bag" so we didn't have to swallow, we still had to chew until the director said "stop camera." Shooting commercials and films isn't always glamorous.

This is a good time to share a cute story about my daddy. On one of my not-so-many visits to see him, I went to the grocery store where he was cutting meat. When I walked up to the butcher counter, I noticed this box of Ritz crackers sitting on his counter. On the back of the box, there was a picture of me that was from the commercial. I said, "Daddy, why do you have this on your counter?" and he replied, "It's your picture from your commercial, and I like to show you off because I'm proud of you." I think that was the first time he ever said that to me.

CHAPTER 14

Irene and Debbie Reynolds

SOMETIME IN THE spring of 1972, I auditioned for the Broadway production of *Irene* starring the fabulous Debbie Reynolds. At the final callback, there were several people in the audience. Sir John Gielgud, the director; Peter Genaro, choreographer; and Jack Lee, the musical director. I heard that Debbie was out there in the dark theatre. After about two hours of dancing and singing, we were lined up across the stage. We stood there for a couple of minutes, and then some people were let go; the rest of us were told to take a half-hour break. A bunch of us went to the Hotel Edison's coffee shop. This was a popular hangout where performers would kill time between auditions and classes. The other popular hangout was the Howard Johnson's on Broadway and 46th Street in Times Square. A quick word about Howard Johnson's: It was very difficult in those days to find part-time work where you could also take time off for auditions. My memory is, Howard Johnson's did hire performers part-time and did give them the time off for auditions. When we returned to the theatre, we were lined up across the stage again, and I believe it was the stage manager who started to give us instructions like "do not cut or color your hair." That's when I raised my hand and asked, "Does this mean we have the job?" Peter Genaro responded, "Of course you've got the job. Didn't we tell Y'all?" In unison we replied "No!" With that, we all let out a collective sigh of relief. I quietly said a "thank you" to God. On the way home I realized that I had this big smile on my face—it lasted for days. I was so proud of myself and wished I could call my momma and tell her I was going to be on Broadway with her favorite movie star, Debbie.

The first day of rehearsals finally came, and we were all gathered in the rehearsal studio talking amongst ourselves when Debbie Reynolds walked into the studio. She was beautiful. She had a glow about her that said "Movie Star." She then said something like "Hello, everyone. I'm so looking forward to working with all of you." And of course we all applauded. Besides the chorus, the principal actors were there also: Monte Markham, who was playing opposite Debbie; movie and stage actress Patsy Kelly, playing Debbie's mom; the funny character actor Billy DeWolf; the famous actress of the stage, screen, and soap star Ruth Warwick; Ted Pugh; Carmen Alvarez; and Janey Sills. The morning was spent with introductions and the week's schedule. After lunch, we started right in with rehearsal. About two weeks into rehearsals Billy got sick and had to drop out. He was replaced with the very capable George S. Irving, who would win a Tony Award, and at some point during rehearsals, Carrie Fisher would also join the company.

After about six weeks of rehearsals, we opened in Toronto, our first out-of-town tryout. There were some bumps in the road in Toronto. There was a hit song from the original 1919 production of *Irene* titled "Alice Blue Gown." Well, there was no Alice Blue Gown because Debbie didn't approve of the first Blue Gown. So she sent for a blue gown from her stock of MGM costumes that she had bought at the studio's auction. I believe it was worn originally by Jane Powell in a movie with Liz Taylor. Also, Debbie was having some voice problems, and the doctor said she would damage her vocal cords if she went on and tried to sing. Although there was an under-rehearsed understudy, the powers-that-be felt that they would have to refund a sold-out audience if they announced that Debbie was not to appear. So somebody came up with an idea. The idea was that Debbie would pantomime her lines and Sir John Gielgud would stand in the wings and recite her dialogue over a microphone. Sound familiar? (*Singin' in the Rain!*) I can't remember what they did as far as the songs go. I do remember that some songs may have been skipped because the chorus was constantly changing backstage for the next dance number. And I do remember that the audience was very disappointed. Debbie did get well, and things did go better for the rest of the Toronto run. However, there was gossip about replacing Sir John. Rumors were that Debbie called her friend Gower Champion and asked if he would take over as director and take us to Broadway.

Philadelphia was our second tryout stop. I think it was in Philly that costume designer Irene Sharif created this incredible Alice blue, floor-length cape, and I do believe that this was when Gower showed up. Although *Irene* had a choreographer, Peter Genaro, Gower wanted to focus on the "Irene" number. On his first day, he started right in on improving it. He envisioned it to be as big and beautiful as was the "Hello Dolly" number, which is one of the quintessential show-stopping production numbers in musical history. We would learn the new changes to the "Irene" number in the daytime, and that night they would go into the show. The next morning he would make more changes to the number and those changes would go into the show that night, and so on. He would build and build until he and Peter were happy. Having done *Hello Dolly* for Gower, I could appreciate his genius. Now I knew he was a perfectionist too. The schedule was exhausting, but Debbie set the rehearsal and performance bar pretty high. She always gave 100 percent at rehearsals and 110 percent in the performance.

It was Christmastime, and Debbie and the producers threw the company a party. There was a moment at the party that I will never forget.

Debbie walked over to me and said: "Dennis, dear." She liked using the endearing word "dear." She went on to tell me that she had been watching me dance at rehearsals and I reminded her of, wait for it, Gene Kelly. She then kissed me on the

cheek and walked away. I cannot tell you how incredibly proud I felt. I really wished that I could call Momma and tell her what Debbie had said. There were many moments in my career when I wished I could share my success with Momma.

Our third and last stop before Broadway was Washington D.C. The show was playing at The National Theatre, but we were rehearsing at The Kennedy Center. Just so you know, Equity's rule is that during out-of-town tryouts the cast could rehearse for five hours during the day with time off before the show that evening, except on days with a matinee. It was at one of these rehearsals at The Kennedy Center that the "Irene" number finally came together. Gower and Peter had been talking over some ideas. At some point Gower walked away to think; he would do this when he was frustrated. While Peter waited for Gower, he spotted one of the girls' hairpieces on the floor next to her dance bag and put it on his head and hid behind one of the pianos. There were four fake pianos in the set of Irene's piano shop. When Gower heard some laughter, he turned around to see Peter pop up from behind the piano with the girl's hairpiece on his head and sing "Irene," then shake his head back and forth singing "la la la la la." It was very funny; Peter was a very funny person. Gower loved it, and it spurred on an idea between the two of how to fix the "Irene" number. It turned out to be a great number. The boys were hidden behind the four fake pianos on stage, and a sad Irene would enter the piano shop at which time the boys would pop up and scare Irene and make her laugh, which led into the "Irene" number—or something like that. At one point in the number, four of the singers rolled their pianos into position over these electric plates in the stage floor. When the cue came these pianos lit up and started playing like old-fashioned player pianos. Then the dancing boys and Debbie climbed up on top of the pianos and did a carefully choreographed dance number with Debbie in the middle.

THE "IRENE" NUMBER

I am second from stage right.

THE "NINTH AVENUE" NUMBER

THE FINALE

I'm first on the left and Carrie is on the floor.

Recording the Cast Album
That's me in the plaid pants, which are bell bottoms.

CHAPTER 15

Finally, *Irene* Makes It to Broadway

***IRENE* STARTED BROADWAY** previews on March 1, 1973, and opened March 13. *Irene* performed at the brand-new Minskoff Theatre located on the sixth floor of the Minskoff Building. When the show moved into the theatre, they were still putting in the audience seats and carpet in the lobby. The dressing rooms were beautiful. The male and female chorus dressing rooms were located on the 7th floor, I believe. They had floor-to-ceiling windows that looked out over West 45th Street. In the older theatres, the dressing rooms usually looked out into an alley. The dressing tables had big mirrors with light bulbs all around them, lots of showers, and a big bathroom. All through the previews, Gower was still tweaking the show. A prologue was added. I remember it was four male singers and four female singers in the number. Usually, it would be just the singers because this song was in tight harmony. All the male and female singers were already in the number, and the musical director, Jack Lee, needed two more voices, so he chose Penny Worth and me because he liked how our voices blended well with the others.

Since the first preview in Toronto, there were lots of changes made to the show. There was a big "dancing fountain" that was used in the fashion-show scene. The tallest girls in the chorus were used as fashion models in one part of the show, and they were staged to walk down the stairs and around the fountain. Unfortunately, the fountain was cut from the show because it kept splashing onto the stage. When Gower came in as the director, there were a lot of changes to the show, not just the "Irene" number. The beautiful song "I'm Always Chasing Rainbows" was taken out of the show and then put back in the show.

There was a scenario to introduce fashion designer Madame Lucy, played by Tony winner George S. Irving, to the high society of New York. Debbie pretended to be this rich Italian Contessa. Debbie's impersonation was hilarious, accent and all. Madame Lucy was said to have designed for the Contessa and would present his fashions at this very fancy garden party given by the very rich Marshall family on their elegant estate. Originally, Debbie was supposed to appear in the Alice blue gown in this fashion show. That was changed: instead, the Contessa wore a long, floor-length, beautiful Alice blue cape. She wanted to stop impersonating the Contessa because she was in love with Donald Marshall, and he with her, and they wanted to end the charade. At a certain point in the fashion show, he removes the cape under which Debbie is wearing her plain dress revealing her as a simple shop girl, not the Contessa she was pretending to be.

On opening night, the dressing rooms were filled with beautiful flowers and lots of gift baskets, champagne, and telegrams with wishes of "break a leg." In the theatre, we don't say "good luck," we say "break a leg." There are a few explanations on why "break a leg." This is the one I like.

Back in the days of shows like *The Ziegfeld Follies*, there were large choruses with many lines of dancers onstage. Each line entered the stage behind different side curtains which defined the different entrance portals from the front of the stage to the back. These curtains are called legs. If a dancer caught the eye of the director because they danced particularly well at a performance, they were moved downstage to the next leg closer to the audience. So to "break a leg" was a move forward closer to the audience where you could be seen better. Hopefully by a big producer or wealthy patron.

The show was perfect on opening night. In the finale when Debbie appeared on stage and bowed, the audience jumped to their feet and gave her a standing ovation. The reviews were wonderful. The opening-night party was at the fashionable Top of the Sixes on Fifth Avenue. I wore a chocolate velvet jacket with a red carnation from one of the flower arrangements I received. The party was so wonderful, and everyone was so beautiful. There were many celebrities there.

I also remember the Sunday morning we recorded the cast album. I hadn't been in a recording studio since *The Red Skelton Show* when we would record songs with the Alan Copeland singers. Although it took from early on a Sunday morning until sometime in the late evening, it was tiring and exciting!

The Tony Awards were held on March 25, 1973, just 12 days after *Irene* opened on Broadway. Debbie was nominated for a Tony Award as Best Actress in a Musical. As Irene, Debbie had to act, sing, and dance. It was disappointing that she did not win the Tony.

Cast members with Bette Midler in the second row and behind her is
Leonard Frey, and then me.

Throughout the run, there were lots of celebrities coming to see
Debbie as Irene. There was the night that Leonard Frye, who I shared a
house with on Fire Island, brought Bette Midler to see *Irene*. Although
I didn't know Bette, we did live just a few blocks from each other in
the Village.

After the show, a group of us gathered to take a picture with Bette and Leonard. Earlier that day I had bought Bette's new album, and it was in my dance bag. So I ran to the dressing room and grabbed the album. Then I gave it to one of the girls down in front, who held it up for the photo. After the picture was taken everyone went their own way. As I sat on the subway going home, it occurred to me that I should have asked Bette to sign my album. Damn! On my way home I stopped at the deli to buy some beer. As I left the store, I saw Bette again, and we said good night and parted. As I put the key in my front door, it hit me. Again, I forgot to ask her to sign my album. Double Damn!!

I don't remember why, but in the late summer the producers turned off the lights at the Minskoff Theatre, where *Irene* was playing on Broadway, and took the entire show to St. Louis, Missouri, to perform in the St. Louis Municipal Opera for a week. The Muni Opera performed in this huge amphitheater under the stars. It has 11,000 seats. Also because the theatre is an amphitheater we couldn't do any matinees, so there were only six shows instead of eight. We stayed at a beautiful hotel. There was a huge pool and a large patio with a grill that made the best hot dogs and hamburgers. We spent our days at the pool where the staff pampered us throughout our stay. One night after the show, Debbie treated the company to an old-fashioned hayride on a horse-drawn wagon with real hay and a fiddler and a harmonica player, so you know songs were sung. Then after the ride, we went into this big barn to square dance. The entire evening was right out of the movies. Leave it to Debbie. The next day we asked Debbie to arrange another square dance, and she did, only we had to do it at the hotel which was fine. It was on our last night in St. Louis before returning to Broadway. As it turned out the Bolshoi Ballet of Russia was booked to follow *Irene* into The Muni Opera. They were also staying at the same hotel, so Debbie invited them to join us in some square dancing. And good for Debbie for ordering extra bottles of vodka.

Debbie and me in St. Louis

CHAPTER 16

A New Year and a New Broadway Show

SOMETIME AROUND THE holiday season, I had this brilliant idea. I was in the upper lobby of the Minskoff Theatre checking out the magnificent view of Times Square. All of a sudden it occurred to me that you could see the ball drop on New Year's Eve from here. What an excellent location for a party. I mentioned this to Debbie, and before I knew it, Debbie made it happen. She had arranged, with the powers-that-be, a New Year's Eve party in the upper lobby after our show. The party was catered, and there was an open bar. Debbie invited her good friend Agnes Moorehead, who was starring on Broadway *in Gigi*, along with the cast of *Gigi* to our party. It was great to be in Times Square on New Year's Eve without being down there in the crowds. Just before midnight, the champagne was poured by the bottles, and these beautiful professional voices sang "Auld Lang Syne" as we welcomed in 1974.

Jane Powell and Ron Hussman

Jane and the Ninth Ave. Fellas.
I'm 2nd from the right

In early 1974, I was cast in the Broadway production of Tom Stoppard's
Jumpers starring Brian Bedford and Jill Clayburgh. In the play, some
of the actors had to also be gymnasts. I didn't want to leave *Irene*, but
this was a straight play on Broadway, which would establish me as a
legitimate Broadway actor. So Debbie made it possible for me to leave
Irene without giving the standard two weeks' notice. On the first day
of rehearsal, I enjoyed having lunch with Jill. She was charming and
lovely. On the second or third day of rehearsals we were building a
pyramid, and I was in the middle on the bottom row. All of a sudden
the pyramid collapsed and I got most of the weight on my lower back.
I was badly injured and had to leave the show. Fortunately, I had a terrific chiropractor who helped me mend quickly. And to tell you how
wonderful Debbie was, she not only made it possible for me to leave

Irene without giving the proper notice, she went to the powers-that-be and made it possible for me to return to *Irene*. Thank God they had not yet found a replacement for me.

In late February of 1974, as per her contract agreement, Debbie left the show, and Jane Powell became the new Irene. Jane was lovely and talented, and I was always a fan of her movies. In September of '74 Debbie returned to play the final week of the show on Broadway. The show closed on September 8th. Debbie took the show on a tour on our way to Los Angeles. Debbie played *Irene* at the Shubert, and then Jane Powell followed her into the Shubert. In Los Angeles, the finale was changed. Irene Sharaff designed this incredible Alice blue gown for Debbie to wear in the finale of *Irene* and then later in her act. The cast would be standing left and right of this large old-fashioned ornate tent. When the curtain came down at the end of the last scene, Debbie was to run into the wings and change out of her costume and into the Alice blue gown and hurry into the tent. Then the curtain would rise and the cast would take their bows. Then the cast would sing "In her sweet little Alice blue gown," and Debbie would enter from the tent for her bows in the brand-new Alice blue gown. Unfortunately, it took too long for Debbie to make the costume change in the wings. I remember Gower and Debbie standing on stage discussing how to make this costume change faster. Suddenly it dawned on me, and without thinking, I spoke up and said, "She can make the costume change in the tent and that way she doesn't have to leave the stage." Debbie and Gower looked at each other and then at me and Debbie said, with all sincerity, "Thank you, dear." I don't remember what Gower said, but I could tell he was happy, and he took my suggestion.

CHAPTER 17

My Return to the West Coast

AT SOME POINT during the Broadway run of *Irene*, Debbie had asked me, and a couple of the other male dancers, to join her nightclub act. So, sometime in the fall of 1974, we went to Hollywood to start rehearsals for Debbie's act. In her show were six male dancers who also sang along with two female singers and one male singer. We rehearsed for three weeks, maybe four. As I remember, we rehearsed the finale for a whole week.

Here's a look at what happened behind the scenes backstage before the curtain went up on stage. We would meet in the afternoon in Debbie's reception room, one of two rooms that encompassed her dressing quarters. We would then sing through the entire show. Then after that Debbie, in her terrycloth robe and turban, would disappear into the second room where she would do her makeup and Pinky would do her hair. And sometime later she would reappear as *Debbie Reynolds*. Amazing! I'm reminded that in Carrie's book *Wishful Drinking*, she talks about her mother's closet being the magical place where Debbie would enter as her mom and emerge as Debbie Reynolds.

In Debbie's show we did a big opening number and then Debbie would take the microphone and step off the stage onto the back of the long dining banquette in her heels. As she made her way around the banquette, she would elegantly lower herself so she could talk to the audience and they could reply into the mic. The audiences loved her. When she made her way back on stage, we boys had already climbed a ladder behind the proscenium and leaned out from the proscenium, in view of the audience, and sang "Irene" which leads into the number. Next Debbie would sing several songs, and we would do more numbers with Debbie. Also, there was a section where she would do her incredible and very funny impersonations.

The finale was fabulous. On stage were two curved mirrored staircases. These were attached to a high platform center stage. The stage was decorated in hanging sheer curtains and a big chandelier above center stage. Debbie was preset on the upper platform center stage, and us boys were placed on the steps left and right of Debbie. The music was "Broadway Melody" from *Singin' in the Rain*. The dancers wore red tuxedos, red top hats, and red tap shoes, and Debbie was in a very similar costume only with lots of sequins on her tux jacket and her satin shorts and fishnet stockings. It was a significantly long tap number, and the singers in the act would sing while we were tapping our feet off. After the standing ovation, Debbie would then sit on a tall stool center stage and end the show singing "Tammy."

Debbie's reception room was always open to her many guests who would come backstage after the show to visit with her. She had a full open bar, and the kitchen of the Desert Inn would roll in a table of appetizers and sandwiches. She loved to visit with her guests. We were always welcome to go into her reception room to eat and drink as she told stories of her off-screen life.

After her guests left, Debbie would excuse herself and go into her inner dressing room to remove the makeup and wig. Then Debbie would return to the reception room in her terrycloth robe and turban and sit with her legs tucked on the side and enjoy a glass of white wine with some of the cast. She loved to tell stories, and we loved to hear them. After an hour or so some cast members would leave. Albert and I usually stayed to the end. This was often around 2 a.m., mind you; our last show ended around midnight, and we would walk Debbie to her bungalow just off the golf course. This bungalow was where Betty Grable and Harry James stayed. The first time I went to that bungalow I was reminded of July 2 in 1973, when Debbie asked me to come to her dressing room after the show. She told me that Betty Grable had just passed away, and she wanted to tell me before I heard it on television.

DEBBIE AND HER GUYS AT THE LONDON PALLADIUM

I'm in the plaid shirt. Debbie is rehearsing her Mae West impersonation, without the wig. She is trying out some new jokes, and I don't remember what she said but it was in the Mae West style of humor and it really caught us off-guard and really made us laugh. I think the look on her face tells a lot.

**Here we are in red tails and top hats with a dancing cane.
Debbie is in the middle, I'm on the far right.**

One of the other wonderful things Debbie would do for us was to reserve the Caesar's Palace yacht. I'm not sure how she got the yacht from Caesar's Palace, but she did. She would have the Desert Inn kitchen prepare food and drink for us to take out on Lake Mead the next morning. There was a captain that came with the yacht, and he would take us out on the lake and find a secluded cove to anchor in for a few hours. It was perfect privacy for those who didn't want a tan line.

Doing Debbie's act was a tough job. When we worked, we worked hard. We played the Desert Inn in Vegas for four weeks straight doing two shows an evening with no full day off. However, we did have the daytime to ourselves. Usually, we went to bed around 7 a.m. That's if we went out to the disco at around 2 a.m. All the casino shows ended late, and no one went out dancing before 2 a.m. I know, you would think that after dancing two full shows you would go home to bed. But no, your adrenalin was so high that sleep was not an option. We ate our big meal after the shows. It was still dark when we went into the restaurant, and when we came out around 6 a.m. you had to put your sunglasses on before you opened the door because the desert morning sun was powerful.

At the end of the four weeks in Vegas, we had a couple of weeks off, with pay. We would then take the act to Reno, Nevada, for a couple of weeks, and later we played Sparks, Nevada, and then back to Vegas. There were no show casinos in Atlantic City at this time. This one time when we were in Reno, Jim Nabors was also doing his act there. Seeing Jim was an excellent opportunity to rekindle our friendship from the CBS FAMILY days. He was a great guy, a good ole southern boy. I remember driving with Albert to his home in Bel Air, California, one Sunday, for dinner. We were listening to the car radio when this talk show about Hollywood stars and their mansions came on the radio. A caller into the show said that they'd heard Jim Nabors had thirteen bathrooms in his mansion. So when I pulled into his large driveway and he came out to welcome us, I asked if he had thirteen bathrooms. His response was "How many do you need?" We went inside his home, and he introduced his friend and gave us a tour of his home. At some point in the afternoon, I mentioned that my daddy was born and raised in the panhandle of Florida and he was a big fan. Jim suggested that I give my daddy a call so he could speak with him. I did make the call, and it was fun to listen to two good ole southern boys chatting on a Sunday afternoon. That's the kind of person Jim was. Also, he was a good cook: he made a delicious spaghetti sauce for dinner.

While in Sparks, NV, I got the chance to pose with
Bertha the elephant. She was very gentle.

In July of 1974, Debbie took us, the act, to London to perform at The London Palladium. That was a big deal. To play The Palladium in London was like playing The Palace in New York City, and we played to sold-out audiences for every performance. The fact that we were even there was due to Debbie. You see they only wanted Debbie, but she insisted that she bring the entire act or she would not go. Opening night was exhilarating. It was sold out and packed with lots of royalty and celebrities. Carrie Fisher made a special appearance. A very proud mother introduced her. She sang two show-stopping hit songs and received a fantastic reception from the audience. Most people had not heard Carrie Fisher sing before. She sang beautifully. A natural, like Momma Cass Elliot who, by the way, was finishing her sold-out performances at the Palladium the night before Debbie opened. Cass left a note to Debbie written on the dressing room mirror in lipstick stating, "If they treat you half as well as they treated me, you'll have the time of your life!" Sadly, after her last performance, Cass Elliot passed away in her sleep.

We played in London for a couple of weeks. After the show closed we had two weeks off before we had to return to the States. A couple of us went to Amsterdam, and then we traveled by train to Paris to meet up with Bob, also in *Irene* and Debbie's act. Paris was everything people say it is. It's wonderful. We had a great time at the Louvre Museum and the park for a lunch of cheese, French bread, and wine. I was told that this is what the Parisians do. Oh, I love Paris! Oh well, the time had come for us to go back to the States and *Irene* in L.A. During the Los Angeles run of *Irene*, I decided to leave New York and give my garden apartment in Greenwich Village to my friend David Thome, and move back to Hollywood. After the Los Angeles run, *The Debbie Reynolds Show* returned to Las Vegas. By the way, the huge billboard in front of the Desert Inn Hotel simply displayed in large white lights *"Debbie."* What more do you need to say!

THE LONDON PALLADIUM

ARGYLL STREET, W.1.

Chairman: SIR LEW GRADE

Deputy Chairman & Managing Director
LOUIS BENJAMIN

General Manager
NEIL BROOKS

OPENS JULY 30th at 7.0 SUBS 6.15 & 8.45 Until Aug 17

LOUIS BENJAMIN and LESLIE GRADE (by arrangement with BILLY MARSH)

Take Great Pride in Presenting

Miss DEBBiE REYNOLDS

IN HER
PREMIERE
PERFORMANCE
IN LONDON

. . . .

WITH HER
ENTIRE COMPANY
DIRECT FROM
LAS VEGAS

and Introducing

CARRIE FISHER

Set Designer
BILL MORRIS

Musical Director
STEVAN DWECK

Vocal Arrangements by
RUDI RENDER

Special Material by
JACK LLOYD

Additional Material by
BRIAN BLACKBURN

Costumes by
RAY AGHAYAN

Staged by
ALEX PLASSCHAERT

Production
Controller
A. J. KNIGHT

During our breaks from Debbie's act, I would audition for commercials. I signed with a great agency that often sent me out on commercial auditions. The commercial I made the most money with was a Nescafé Instant Coffee. I played a sailor on a tugboat drinking coffee from a glass mug shaped like the globe. I was in the hallway one day when I heard the introduction to my Nescafé commercial. I ran into the living room to see my commercial for the first time. What I saw was the tugboat passing in front of the Statue of Liberty, only we shot the commercial in Long Beach, California. I was confused for a second until I realized they had superimposed the Statue of Liberty. The Nescafé commercial ran for a long time. And there were more commercials to come.

MY NESCAFÉ COFFEE COMMERCIAL

I was booked on an Arthur Treacher's Fish n' Chips. It was a cute commercial and every dancer in Hollywood wanted to get this job. Well, I did get the job. We were costumed in yellow rain slickers like in *Singin' in the Rain*. There were three of us, two guys and one girl. We sang and danced, just like in *Singin' in the Rain*. Next, I danced in the film *New York, New York* starring Robert DeNiro and Liza Minnelli directed by Martin Scorsese. The score was by a good friend of mine John Kander and the late Fred Ebb, also a friend. I will never forget the first day I walked onto the studio lot. It was still called the MGM Studios at that time. It was thrilling to walk down the streets of this famous film studio where so many movies I love were filmed. We filmed *New York, New York* on the same sound stage where *The Wizard of Oz* was filmed along with *Singin' in the Rain* and many Judy Garland movies. Liza used the same dressing room her mother used for so many movies. We filmed a couple of dance numbers with Liza, and some of them never made it into the movie. Oh well, it was a joy to go to work for all those weeks at this legendary film studio. At that time Liza was married to Jack Haley, Jr., the son of Jack Haley who played the Tin Man in *The Wizard of Oz*. So Dorothy's daughter and the Tin Man's son got married, which made Dorothy and the Tin Man in-laws. Weird? Not in Hollywood!

CHAPTER 18

A Chorus Line: My Life Changes

IN JULY OF 1975, *A Chorus Line*, conceived, directed, and choreographed by Michael Bennett, opens on Broadway. It was a huge hit and the talk of the town. The critics loved this show, and so did the audiences. Not since *Oklahoma* had a Broadway musical had such an impact and changed the face of musical theatre like *A Chorus Line*. When I was back in New York, I got to see this incredible play when it was still Off-Broadway. As I sat in The Newman Theatre, I was mesmerized by the presentation happening on stage. I have never had an experience in the theatre like the one I was having at that moment. From the beginning of the play, when in the dark a lone piano plays a six-note introduction, to the very last high kicks at the end of the play, it was evident that Michael had created more than just a Broadway musical. *A Chorus Line* would be awarded the Pulitzer Prize for Drama and nine Tony Awards. Michael had a lot of help from assistant Bob Avian, dance captain Baayork Lee, Marvin Hamlisch, Ed Kleban, James Kirkwood, and Nick Dante, and all the dancers who participated in the taping sessions offering their life stories. All of them took us on a ride through the lives of 17 performers and the director. With the last note in the piano intro the stage lights lit up the bare stage, revealing many dancers facing upstage into the mirrors learning dance steps from the director/choreographer. We are now watching an audition in progress. The performers are auditioning for a Broadway musical, and before the end of the play, they will open their hearts and souls to the director—anything to get this job. The energy on stage from the dancers was overpowering, leaving the audience sitting on the edge of their seats. After the director eliminated all but 17 performers, the audience sat back in their seats having just experienced what a real dance audition was like. The 17 who remained stood on a white line painted on the floor of the stage. The director, who was now a disembodied voice from the back of the theatre, instructed them to step out of line one at a time and give their name, when they were born, and where. Already this was like no other audition I had attended. For the next 90 minutes, the auditioners would willingly reveal their dreams, loves, and fears from their adolescence to adulthood.

For those who don't know, *A Chorus Line* was created from a collection of tapes of dancers talking about how they started dancing and why they started dancing, about their early lives and their careers in show business. There were two tapings, and both were kept a big secret. The two taping sessions ultimately spawned the six-week workshop produced by Joseph Papp and the Public Theatre. Michael asked for a second workshop because he knew that he was onto something. As a result of the two workshops, an Off-Broadway production of *A Chorus Line* was produced in the Newman Theatre at the Public Theatre. Because of the rave reviews and demand for tickets, *A Chorus Line* quickly transferred to Broadway. Who knows? Maybe if I had taken Michael up on his offer I might be up on that stage instead of sitting in the audience. I identified with so many of their stories, and I wondered what role I would play. But there wasn't a particular role that I identified with the most. Before the end of the performance, I had resolved that I had to get into this play—somehow.

After the play, I wondered if the general audience could identify with *A Chorus Line* considering its story is set in the theatre and about theatre people. I wondered if the average person not associated with the theatrical arts would understand how brilliantly Michael told these many stories within the guise of an audition for a Broadway show. How Michael with the help of Tharon Musser, lighting designer, communicated to the audience what was the reality on stage and what were their internal thoughts. My favorite memory of my first time seeing this play was how Michael shared with the audience how dancers learn musical numbers through repetition. In the "One Singular Sensation" number, Michael laid it all out, giving the audience a revelation. When the show opened I got my answer: *A Chorus Line* definitely has a universal appeal. Sometime after the show opened on Broadway Michael Bennett and his assistant, Bob Avian, came out to Los Angeles to hold auditions for the upcoming production of *A Chorus Line* in Los Angeles. So of course, I auditioned. It was on Saturday and Sunday. We danced for hours and sang our audition songs. The next day was the callbacks. Again we danced and sang. After the audition was over, Michael said to me that my audition was great, but my personality didn't suit a particular character in the play. I thanked Michael and told him that I agreed with him. *A Chorus Line* was now dead for me. It made me Sad!

I believe it was in May 1976 when all but two of the original cast members left the Broadway cast and joined the now Los Angeles company. They first opened in San Francisco and played for a couple of weeks before moving to Los Angeles. After the show opened at the

Shubert Theatre in Los Angeles, one of the original cast members, Ron Kuhlman, gave his notice to leave the show. An audition notice went out to the casting offices. One day my agent, Joseph, called to tell me that he had submitted my picture and resume for *A Chorus Line* and they wanted to see me. I didn't expect to get an audition because the original Don Kerr was a tall, fair-haired, all-American type and I am not. You see, the word was out that Michael was typecasting, meaning someone who looked the part.

On the day of the audition, I showed up at the Shubert Theatre in Century City. Most of Century City used to be all of the back lots of Twentieth Century Fox Studios. Now it's a suburb of Los Angeles. Like most audition calls there were lots of people there. Lots of the auditioners were tall and fair-haired, all-American looking. Like the first audition Michael held in L.A. many months earlier, we learned the ballet combination and the jazz combination from the show. There was a cut, and then those who stayed sang. Another cut and they thanked those of us who were left. A few days later my agent called me with a time slot for a callback audition. That was good news, and maybe *A Chorus Line* wasn't dead for me after all.

There were a couple of callbacks. Near the end of the final callback, Michael started to eliminate from the few who'd made it that far. Finally, all but two of us had been eliminated. So this is the final moment. One of us will be eliminated, and one of us will leave this theatre as the new Don Kerr. So there we stood in the wings, myself and I don't remember who, but at that moment it could have been Santa Claus. My heart was racing. I never expected to get this far because I was not the right type for this role. Anyway, Michael was center stage, and we were in the wings stage right. Michael calls the other person to join him on stage. I kept telling myself to keep breathing. Michael said something that made that person very happy because he hugged Michael as he said "thank you, Michael" and left the stage. My heart sank: I knew it was over.

Then Michael calls me to come on stage. He put his arm around my neck and walked me upstage and said: "I've got to hand it to you, Dennis, you are Don Kerr, you've got the job." Instantly my knees went weak, and all I could say was, "Are you kidding me, Michael? Oh my God, thank you, Michael, thank you!" We hugged, and Michael said I would be contacted soon to sign my contract. I thanked him again, and as I left the stage I realized that in that one moment my life had changed for the better. I guess I convinced Michael, after all, that I was the right person for the role. Before I left the theatre, I found out that Michael was sending the other person to the London cast. I didn't know he needed to hire another person and I was thrilled to be hired for the Los Angeles company. On the drive home all I could think about was, Oh My God, I'm in *A Chorus Line*.

Now the unpleasant part. I had to call Debbie Reynolds to tell her the good news about *A Chorus Line* and the bad news: I would not be returning to her act. Well, she was not happy to hear that I was leaving her act. However, she was happy for my success and wished me the best. I would miss seeing Debbie almost every day. She always had a smile on her face, a "hello dear," and a kiss for my cheek.

I started rehearsals for *A Chorus Line* with Linda Dangcil, who was hired after me. I didn't know Linda before I met her at rehearsals, but we immediately became friends. When Linda was a little girl, she appeared in the original Broadway production of *Peter Pan* with Mary Martin. Also, she danced in the film version of *West Side Story*. Some might remember her as Sister Ana on *The Flying Nun* with Sally Fields. She had a nice career. Linda and I became good friends. I loved her tender gentleness and her support of me during the rehearsal period. I am sorry to say that Linda passed away in 2009. She is truly missed. Baayork Lee, who created the role of Connie Wong in *A Chorus Line*, was the dance captain and taught us the show.

Baayork was in the original Broadway production of *The King and I* when she was five, and Fran Liebergall, the music director and assistant to Marvin Hamlisch, taught us all of the music, and all this in only two weeks, maybe three.

During rehearsals, I remember trying on my finale costume for the first time. I looked into the mirror and thought, this is the most beautiful costume I have ever worn and what an honor to wear this gorgeous costume, designed by Theoni Aldredge.

The Los Angeles Company of *A Chorus Line*
"The Line." I'm first on the far left.

This cartoon was on the front page of the Sunday Entertainment section of the *Los Angeles Times* with an article by Daniel Sullivan about *A Chorus Line*. The characters are out of place; in the play I'm the first character on stage right.

Finally, opening night came. Actually, it was a matinee. As we were waiting to take our places on stage, we would hold hands in a circle and chant "Nam Myoho Renge Kyo"—a Buddhist chant for, in this case, a great show. Remember we don't say "good luck" in the theatre.

It's my first performance, and I remember standing there "on the line" after the opening number. There I was holding up my 8x10 headshot in front of my face and feeling very proud. I was right where I belonged. Near the end of the play before the finale the character Paul falls, as scripted, and hurts his bad knee and is carried off. Then, there was a moment of "what if it was me?" The director looks at all of us and says, "What do you do when you can't dance anymore?" As I pondered his question I realized I had never thought there might be a time when I wouldn't be able to dance, not even after the two surgeries. And as we sang "What I Did for Love" it all came to me—the true meaning of the lyrics "the gift was ours to borrow," and what it meant to put yourself on the line, whether it's for a job or a loving relationship. If you don't participate in life, it will pass you by.

A Chorus Line was a big hit in Los Angeles as it was in New York. The Hollywood celebrities were coming every night. Some came several times. There were many parties. Sammy Davis Jr. and his wife Altovise, who was also a dancer, threw a big party for the entire cast. It was at their home in Bel Air, the other Beverly Hills, and the Davises were warm and hospitable.

One afternoon between the matinee and evening show, I was Christmas shopping and ran into John Travolta. I knew John from New York when we both were doing Broadway shows. He was always so nice. We often ate at the same restaurant, not the same table, between matinee and evening shows. There was another time when we bumped into each other. It was at one of the television studios where we both were shooting something. I was in the hallway on a break when we spotted each other. I was surprised to see him in L.A. I asked what he was doing out in California, and he said he was doing a pilot for a possible television series. I asked John the name of the show, and he replied, "*Welcome Back, Kotter.*" And the rest is history.

Although the L.A. run of *A Chorus Line* was successful, we closed after 2 ½ years and moved to the Shubert Theatre in Chicago for a sit-down run. A sit-down run is an unlimited run. I had played the Shubert Theatre in Chicago before with *Hello Dolly*. It was cold then, and it was still cold. The day after we arrived in Chicago we went to the rehearsal studios to meet with Michael and Bob. Michael had us sit on the floor in a circle as he did in the first taping session that eventually led to the development of *A Chorus Line*. He then said, "Why did you start dancing? Let's start with you and go around the room." The questions kept coming for a couple of hours. Michael somehow found a parallel of sorts between you and your character and the show. This process had a significant positive impact on the cast. I learned a lot about all the characters and how they were developed into the show. I learned that my character Don Kerr was a combination of Michael's early beginnings as a dancer and Andy Bew, who was a dancer and a part of the original tape recordings session.

It was during these rehearsals that Michael told us that we were all special because we were using our God-given talents and creating a career, doing what makes us happy and making a living doing it.

Around the Easter holiday, we had a severe snowstorm. It was freezing and windy. It had been freezing since we arrived about four months ago. I couldn't take the weather any longer, and the arthritis in my knee was killing me. I walked into the stage manager's office and handed him my two-weeks' notice to leave the show. I just wanted to go back to Hollywood and be warm and buy a home. I had saved a lot of money from my commercials and their residuals. The residuals are payments the actor receives every time the commercial is played on TV. Along with that and my salary from *A Chorus Line*, I was ready to buy a home. Good-bye to cold Chicago.

CHAPTER 19

At Home, Poolside

I DID BUY a home with a pool in the backyard where there were beds of flowers and citrus trees. It was a California ranch with three bedrooms. I loved my new home. It felt great to be a homeowner. I rested for a while by the poolside with a beer in my hand or on the table next to me. If I wasn't resting on the patio, I was resting on a float in the pool. I spent a lot of time in the pool. It was a nice-sized pool with a diving board and I loved to dive. I enjoyed entertaining my friends poolside—there were lots of pool parties. *A Chorus Line* is a strenuous show and demanding on the body with eight shows a week. Having a break from that schedule was nice. I remember waking up one morning and not feeling any pain in my body for the first time in a long time.

My First House

I did go back to work, eventually. I did a commercial here and there. I performed in an industrial show in Long Beach for one of the big beer companies, and I stayed aboard the *Queen Mary*, which is permanently docked in Long Beach, California. Then I did another industrial show in Acapulco, Mexico. I loved Acapulco. The cast stayed at a fabulous hotel in the cliffs overlooking the beautiful Pacific Ocean. It was the first time I stayed in a hotel where you could swim up to the bar—how civilized. In 1979, I was invited to do a production of *A Chorus Line* in Hawaii; my friend Baayork Lee was directing. Hawaii was wonderful. This was a great gig because we did no matinees, which left the days open for beach time and touring the island of Oahu. Hawaii is a paradise. The people there welcomed us with open arms. We made friends with The Brothers Cazimero, who were big singing stars in Hawaii, and their friend Lienaala. I hope I have the name right. She was a famous hula dancer and teacher. They and their friends threw us a real luau, pig in the ground and all. The Hawaiians are very loving. On our last performance, Lienaala stood in the wings and, before we stepped out on stage to take our bow in the finale, she placed a beautiful lei around our necks. The audience went crazy when they saw us with the leis over our finale costumes.

Just before the show closed, the casting directors for *Hawaii Five-O* saw the show and offered me a small part. I played "Man on the Beach."

I was a surfer and carried a surfboard. As I came running out of the water, I saw a woman in distress on the sand. I ran over to her, and as I helped her to sit up, I said, "Hey lady, are you OK?" to which she replied, "Get help." And I said, "Sure, lady," and then I ran out of the shot. That was it. It was a tough shoot only because the beach was just off the highway and not a beach used for sunbathing or swimming and especially not surfing. There were a lot of rocks in the water, which hurt my feet. The waves were somewhat strong, which kept knocking me over and causing me to lose the surfboard. Not fun but I was very grateful for the gig and the residuals to come.

In the spring of 1980, when *A Chorus Line*'s tour was returning to California, Michael called and said he knew I didn't want to go on tour but would I do the show in Hollywood and San Francisco for a few weeks. So I agreed. In this company was a wonderful person named Rita O'Connor. She was playing the role of Sheila in *A Chorus Line*. Rita also did a lot of Broadway shows like *Cabaret*, *Coco* with Katherine Hepburn, and *Follies*, to name a few. Rita and I became close friends. It was Rita who, at the taping sessions of *A Chorus Line*, said life at home wasn't always good but "everything was beautiful at the ballet"—so Rita told me. While we were in San Francisco, we flew down to Los Angeles on our day off and shot the television special *Baryshnikov on Broadway*, also starring Liza Minnelli. Mikhail wanted to do the finale of *A Chorus Line*, and so he joined the "line" with the rest of us and performed the finale. When we were called to the set to shoot the number, Rita, who had long beautiful red hair, decided to make a quick stop at the hair room for one last hair check. She grabbed this plastic spray bottle and gave her hair a couple of spritzes. As she made her way to the sound stage, her hair began to wilt. As it turned out, what she'd thought was hairspray was actually oil. I don't think too many people noticed because everyone had their eyes on Mikhail Baryshnikov.

It was not long after when late one night Michael called. My friend David Thome, who was playing Don Kerr on Broadway, was leaving to do *Dreamgirls*. Michael said that he needed me to come to New York and join the Broadway company as Don Kerr. That was an offer too good to turn down, and you don't say no to Michael. So I leased my house, which I would eventually sell, and rented an apartment on the Upper West Side of Manhattan.

CHAPTER 20

Back on Broadway

THE NIGHT I joined *A Chorus Line* on Broadway was a long-awaited dream come true. I was pleased with my performance, and it felt like home to perform in the Shubert Theatre. After the show, when the audience left, I stood on stage looking out into the semi-darkened auditorium. Remembering my childhood dream, an epiphany overwhelmed me: there comes a moment in life when all the dreams, prayers, and hard work come together. That moment for me was now.

I AM IN *A CHORUS LINE* ON BROADWAY! Momma, I made it to the Big Time!

Me as Don Kerr singing "you know, the nightclub union"

I never got tired of walking out of the stage door with other cast members and seeing a crowd of fans seeking our autographs and wanting to take pictures with us. The holidays arrived, and I had forgotten how beautiful New York could be during this time of the year. There were lots of parties. I had been invited to a New Year's Day brunch by Troy, who was in the show and dance captain. Troy lived across the street, and he was famous for his garlic burgers. There were several of Troy's friends present. There was Troy's partner, Guy, and Debbie, and Alan. And then there was John!!! John and Troy grew up together in California.

John was a successful model and seeing him you knew why. He worked in Paris, Milan, New York, and California. He was tall and very handsome. We hit it off right away and were instantly attracted to each other. He was nothing like I'd thought he might be, being so good-looking. He was warm and had a sweet innocence about him. John came home with me that night, which was the beginning of a very loving relationship.

As the weeks passed, we became more than just best friends—we were inseparable. We spent every day and night together. About two months later he moved in with me, which was the beginning of our lifelong partnership. This partnership would last for fourteen years, until he prematurely left this world in 1993.

Living in our building were other people connected to the company of *A Chorus Line*. There was Deborah, Lois, and R.J., who were "on the line," meaning in the cast, and one other person from *A Chorus Line* who was a spotlight electrician. It was like having a little family in the building. Speaking of family, when you are a part of a Broadway cast or any cast of a show, you become a family. That's because of all the time you spend together during the rehearsal period. And of course, the time you spent together for the run of the show, which could last for years.

After John moved in with me a friend of ours, Debbie, who I'd met at the same time I met Alan and John, also moved into the building, adding to the family. Sometimes after the show, some of the cast would come over to our apartment, and I would cook. It was a lot of fun. It was usually the same group. Sometimes it would be Tracy, Danny, Debra who lived down the hall, sometimes Bebe. There were lots of parties on the roof of our building. We would do Memorial Day, Fourth of July, and Labor Day, and for no reason at all, Let's Have A Party Day. John and I would barbeque, and the others would bring food and drink. A good time was had by all.

There were nights when the cast of *A Chorus Line* would be invited to Studio 54, a very popular dance club in New York City. It was also very popular with celebrities. Not just anyone would be allowed to pass by the red velvet rope and enter the club. But when you are in *A Chorus Line*, you are always invited inside. There were so many events and celebrations of some kind, and it always involved lots of champagne and some ... well that's all I'm going to say.

In February 1981 the Broadway company of *A Chorus Line* was invited to perform at President Reagan's first Governors Ball. Before we could accept, we all had to have a background check. We all passed so off to Washington D.C. we went. It was very exciting to drive onto the grounds of the White House. We had a rehearsal on the portable stage in the East Room. Then we checked into the beautiful hotel across the street. Later that evening after the cocktail party and dinner, everyone gathered into the East Room for the entertainment. We performed the finale. After the show, the President and First Lady came up on stage to shake our hands. After we got back to our hotel, we had our party. Early the next morning we flew back to New York and went right to the theatre to do a matinee. Boy that was tough considering we only had a few hours of sleep. Talk about bad timing! Speaking about bad timing. I don't remember why I was at the Minskoff Rehearsal Studios, which no longer exist—it was probably a commercial audition—but I do remember I was in the lobby of the studios when Bob Fosse came out of one of the rooms and walked into the lobby to make a phone call (no cell phones back then). I had auditioned for Bob in the past so he recognized me and said hello. While he was waiting for someone to pick up on the other end of the phone he looked back at me and said, "Are you working?" I said, "Yes." He replied with a disappointed "Damn." When he started to speak into the phone I turned around so I was not staring at him or eavesdropping on his conversation, but I did hear him say on the phone that he needed to replace a male dancer. Then I thought to myself that perhaps I should ask Bob why he wanted to know if I was working—was he going to offer me a job? I decided that I should ask, but unfortunately, when I turned back around, he was going into the hall and disappeared. Damn! Opportunities in show business can come and go quickly.

It was sometime in the spring, I think, that I started rehearsals for the movie *Annie*. We rehearsed at 890 Broadway, which Michael Bennett owned. There were a lot of dancers hired for this movie. Initially, I did not audition for the film because of my show schedule with *A Chorus Line*. Later as shooting began, they hired additional dancers for the Radio City Music Hall segment. The movie company agreed to shoot around the show schedule of the dancers who were in a Broadway show. It was a tight schedule for us but another paycheck. The Music Hall dance segment was going to be a considerable extravaganza involving 30-plus dancers, the Rockettes, and Grace played by Ann Reinking.

The scene began with the extras dressed in ushers' uniforms and lined up in the lobby to welcome the Daddy Warbucks' entourage into the theatre. Annie with Sandy and Grace took their seats. On stage are three old-time movie sets. Stage right was a north pole set with a team of huskies, center stage was a pirate ship, and stage left was a desert scene. I was costumed as Rudolph Valentino.

As the scene on stage started the huskies begin to howl, which sets off Sandy, who then runs down the aisle to the stage with Grace in pursuit. Somehow she gets caught up into the scene, which leads into a big dance with the dancers, and then the Rockettes do their thing, kicking and kicking. It was all very MGM. I understand that a lot of what we shot was edited out. If a movie is running long, the first to be cut are the musical dance numbers. This is probably why I have not seen the whole movie.

I believe it was in 1982 that I suffered another injury to my bad knee during the finale of *A Chorus Line*. As I limped off the stage, I knew my knee was bad. The next day I saw my doctor. He said I would probably need more surgery and that I should not dance for several months and I should consider giving up dancing. I couldn't believe what I was hearing. I knew this meant I would probably have to leave the show, which was perhaps the best thing for me now anyway. I had been in the show for several years, and the strenuous dancing was putting a lot of strain on my knee. I started missing shows because of the pain. So, after a lot of thought I made the heartbreaking decision to leave *A Chorus Line*.

CHAPTER 21

Return To California and
A Chorus Line Gala

SINCE I COULDN'T work and John's schedule was very flexible, we decided we would make a cross-country trip and visit family and friends along the way. So we went up the block and rented a car for the month. We drove down the East Coast and stopped in Florida to visit my daddy and my brother Randy. After Momma's death, my daddy moved back to the Edenfield farm in the panhandle of Florida. Then we drove across the Gulf states to New Orleans, where we stayed for a few days. From there we headed west and visited many of the national parks, which were so beautiful and fascinating. We finally made it to Los Angeles. We visited one of my best friends Mick and his partner Tim and others before we drove up the coast on Highway 1, which is the scenic route that hugs the coastline. The scenic views were breathtaking with every curve in the road. We stopped in Santa Barbara to visit friends of ours, David and Anastasia, who lived on a large avocado farm. We stayed with them for a few days. Santa Barbara is so beautiful. Our next stop was San Francisco for a couple of days. San Francisco is always an exciting experience. It was now time to head east and back home.

It was not long after we returned home that we discussed the possibility of leaving New York and moving to California. I knew that I could work out there as an actor doing commercials, and John was sure he could also work out there since he started his successful modeling career in Hollywood. So we gave the landlord notice and started packing. Too bad I had sold my house in California a couple of years earlier.

John and I relocated to Hollywood in the spring of 1983. We found this terrific house to rent in the hills of Hollywood. From our deck just off the den, we could see the Hollywood sign, and we were not far from my friend Mick's house. John did some modeling for International Male and other clients, and I also did some commercials.

In September of 1983, *A Chorus Line* broke the record for the longest-running musical on Broadway. As he has always done, Michael went all out in a big way to celebrate this unprecedented accomplishment. An invitation was sent out to three-hundred-plus members of *A Chorus Line*, present and past companies, to participate in the celebration at the Shubert Theatre on Broadway. Three hundred thirty-two members accepted, including me. After a year of recuperating from my fall in the finale, I felt I could pull off a couple performances since I wasn't doing the full show. I found out later that my participation in the Gala was dancing the tap combination and the finale.

Michael did a very smart thing the night before rehearsals were to start. He gave a big party so that we all had a chance to come together and hug and kiss and reminisce, as most of us had not been together for years. It was truly the happiest party I have ever enjoyed, to date. Walking up to the theatre the next morning, I noticed that the names of those who ever appeared in *A Chorus Line* were scrolling across the theatre marquee. How cool is that! Michael had this very tall ladder set in the audience, which he climbed and started with the obligatory Thank-You's and continued with instructions on how the week ahead would unfold. We all received a schedule of the rehearsals and we were given subway tokens to get to and from the rehearsals. Michael also announced who would be in what part of the Gala. The original Broadway company and the existing Broadway company would participate in the opening of the show. The rest of us would be assigned to the remaining companies: the original casts of the national company, the international company, the bus and truck company, and the Chicago company. He went on to explain what company would participate in what part of the play. For instance, the opening of the play would be the current Broadway company. Near the end of the opening number when they moved forward toward the white line downstage, there was a blackout and that company exited. When the lights came back on, the original company was standing on the line holding their 8x10 photos in front of their faces.

September 29, 1983 – Performance 3,389 of *A Chorus Line*

At the gala performance, the audience went crazy and leaped to their feet with cheers and applause that went on forever—so it seemed. This was Michael's ingenious way to start the play with the original cast: the people who'd participated in the workshops and the creation of *A Chorus Line*.

Michael and those who were a part of the planning of this Gala Presentation did a brilliant job. What was particularly outstanding to me was how Michael presented the Cassie scene "Music And The Mirror." Donna McKechnie, the original Cassie and Tony Award winner, played the scene and song leading into the dance. Shortly into the dance five mirrors on stage were flown out of sight, revealing seven other Cassies who danced in tandem with Donna. This was fabulous! The character Paul has a heart-wrenching monologue about his early life and hiding his homosexuality. This monologue started with the original Paul, and then a group of actors who had played the role of Paul enters on stage and like a Greek chorus echoes what Paul is saying. Chilling and touching at the same time.

The scene called the alternative scene, regarding "What do you do if you can't dance anymore?," was performed by the foreign company, speaking in their native language. Interesting!

The day of the Gala, the city was abuzz with anticipation. This was the day *A Chorus Line* would break the record and become the longest-running Broadway musical in history. The performances were flawless. There were two performances—one in the afternoon and the evening performance, which was black tie only. The evening performance audience also got to go to the Gala Party after the play. Since there were so many performers participating in the Gala we had to dress into our costumes next door at the adjoining theatre, the Booth. There was a large screen on stage at the Booth so we could watch what was happening on stage at the Shubert. That way we knew when to go next door for our participation on stage. On my way to the Shubert I saw Mildred Natwick of whom I'm a big fan, and I had to let her know. She was charming and introduced her friend Helen Hayes. Wow!

Because there were 332 performers, they had to add additional supports under the stage. The reason being that Michael had all 332 performers on stage for the end of the finale. The finale started with the original cast, then the other companies were added into the finale. Near the end of the finale, those performers who were dancing in the aisles ran up on stage until all 332 were doing the high kicks. The audience erupted into a standing ovation! The "bravos" and applause were so loud I thought the roof of the Shubert Theatre was going to fly off. Again it seemed as if it lasted forever. Then Michael walked onstage and did his best to quiet the audience's applause and cheers. When he could speak he introduced and invited the producer Joseph Papp, the entire artistic team, the dance captains, Wardrobe Mistress Alyce Gilbert, and Conductor Don Pippin with the orchestra, all to join us on stage. After the performance there was an incredible party held in the tented Shubert Alley. This party was absolutely fantastic. So many celebrities. Imagine Paul Newman and Joanne Woodward telling you how wonderful you were in the play! And there were many more congrats from other celebrities and guests.

After I returned home in Hollywood an old friend from New York, Scott, was visiting and called to see if we could get together, so I invited him over for dinner. At dinner, he told us that he was working as a cruise director for American Hawaii Cruise Lines. He mentioned that his assistant was taking some time off and Scott needed an assistant cruise director, and would I consider going to Hawaii for six weeks. John spoke up and said that I should do it. I told Scott that I couldn't go away for six weeks and leave John alone. We were still at the stage in our relationship where we were inseparable. Then Scott said that he was also looking for a person for the shore excursion position. We both thought about it for a second and then said, "Aloha to Hollywood!" We found someone to stay in our home, and John's sister took care of our kitty while we were away in Hawaii.

In November we boarded the *SS Constitution* in Oahu and went to sea. The ship only sailed around the Hawaiian Islands and docked in ports on the big island of Hawaii, Maui, and Kauai. We set sail on Saturday morning and returned to Oahu on the next Saturday. The islands were magificent, a true paradise. I enjoyed being the assistant cruise director and it turned out that I was good at it. The cruise director and the assistant were the "go-to people" for the passengers because we were there to greet them when they boarded the ship. We hosted the Captain's Ball on the first night at sea, we hosted all the entertainment and events and served as Masters of Ceremonies for all the shows where we also had to sing a number or two. I was informed that I had to come aboard with at least four songs with instrumental charts for the band. Dick, the husband of my friend Linda Dangcil from *A Chorus Line*, was an excellent music arranger, and he offered to create my music charts for free. Usually, these charts would have cost me hundreds of dollars.

John liked his job also. He got to escort all the tours on shore, so he got to see everything that was there to see. After several weeks, Scott, the cruise director, left his job and I was asked to take over as cruise director. At this time there were only two weeks left before we were to leave the ship and go back to Hollywood. John and I discussed staying a little longer. I agreed to stay for a few months, which turned into almost six months at sea, and I was loving it. I realized that if I was going to salvage my career, I needed to go back to New York. So we said, "Aloha, Hawaii!"

We went back to Hollywood and packed up our belongings to be shipped back to New York. On the way back to New York we made a side trip to New Orleans. My friend and mentor Jack had taken over Al Hurt's nightclub in the French Quarter and renamed it Le Moulin Rouge. He asked if I would consider staying in New Orleans for a few months and join the cast of his show at Le Moulin Rouge. I owed Jack a lot for making me a better dancer and encouraging me to go to New York and for all his support throughout my career, so I said yes to a couple of months. It was fun living in the French Quarter. John was working for a travel agency and I was doing Jack's show at night. I enjoyed doing the show, the cast was fun to work with, and there were only four of us. After the show, many nights were spent sitting on the balcony of one of the bars talking with my friend Ricky, who was also in the show. We would talk about producing our own show sometime in the future, maybe. I briefly thought about bringing my years of experience back home to New Orleans and starting a theatre company.

However, it didn't take me long to realize that New Orleans was more interested in sports and there were a couple of established theatre companies in New Orleans already. So I scrapped that idea and decided that it was definitely time to get my butt back to New York City.

CHAPTER 22

New York: Back Where I Belong and a New Career Transition

ONCE WE WERE back in New York, we moved to trendy Park Slope in Brooklyn. John took a job with a tour group that did safaris to Africa. I was hired to perform in a television special titled *Night of 100 Stars 2*. This was a Tribute to The Actors Fund of America, which offers unparalleled support for the theatrical community. There were more than 300 stars presented on stage at the historic Radio City Music Hall. We performed in many musical numbers with so many stars. I had the honor of tumbling with the Gold-winning gymnastic team from the 1984 Olympics, while The Pointer Sisters sang their hit "Jump." It makes sense! There was a significant musical segment that started with a musical number starring Dick Van Dyke. John Kander and Fred Ebb, the hugely successful writing team of Broadway musicals, wrote this terrific song about an actor Conrad Cantzen. He bequeathed his estate to the Actors Fund of America so that actors could afford to buy a new pair of shoes. With the new shoes, they would look more successful when they auditioned. Albert Stephenson choreographed a great number for us, and the number led into the second part of this big musical dance segment. There was a tap section with celebrities who could tap. This led to several celebrities who danced, and each had a solo. The last star to appear in this number was Ginger Rogers escorted by Dick Van Dyke, who I'd worked with a few years back on his own television special. Now going back to the end of the song and dance that we did with Dick Van Dyke, as the stage lights dimmed on stage left, Dick exited the stage to make his costume change for his appearance with Ginger Rogers. I was in the wings about to enter on stage when Nikki, one of Albert's assistants, approached me and told me that if, for some reason, Dick did not make it to the wings on time to escort Miss Rogers, I was going to have to do it. Oh no, now I was really nervous. Thank God Dick made it on time.

A Chorus Line at the Pioneer Theatre Company in Salt Lake City, Utah
Debra played Cassie and I was Zack.

After that job, I did a production of *A Chorus Line* in Utah and played the role of Zach, the director in the play. Patty d'Beck was directing. Patty and I did the show together on Broadway. And then I did another production of *A Chorus Line* in Ohio. In the first week of rehearsals, John called to tell me that my daddy had passed away. I took a couple of days off to attend his funeral. After I returned to New York, my friend Patty called me again to do *A Chorus Line*. She was going to direct/choreograph a production at a small summer stock theatre in upstate New York, The Mac-Haydn Theatre. She wanted me to assist her and then take over on the last few days while she went on to a previous engagement. After *A Chorus Line* opened the producers, Linda and Lynn, took me to lunch and said that they liked the way I worked with the cast and crew and asked if I would direct/choreograph a show for them next summer. I said yes. They said they would call next year in the spring to talk details.

The spring of 1986 arrived, and I went to Saugatuck, Michigan, to choreograph *Mame* in this cute barn theatre. I love barn theatres; I can't look at a barn and not wonder if it could become a theatre. Well, you already know that from the Mouseketeers' story earlier in this book. I loved choreographing *Mame*, the cast was great, and I really liked working with the producer, Paul, who also directed. Saugatuck is a wonderful town along Lake Michigan's shore. It is an artsy community of gay and gay-friendly people and the twin town to Douglas, Michigan. Together the towns offered terrific art galleries, restaurants, and boutique shops to enjoy.

But what sticks out in my memories about Saugatuck is how wonderful my host family was. The actress who played Vera, a lead role, was kind enough to open her home to me. One afternoon we all were on the back deck of their house having a picnic when suddenly the wind picked up, and things started to fly around, and the sky was getting darker. At that point I realized we were all being escorted into their basement. Once safely inside and the door securely shut the dad turned on the radio, and we heard that a tornado had touched down in their neighborhood. Well, my heart began to race as the noise became unbearable. I glanced over to see the boys and dad playing race cars, undisturbed by what was happening outside. I guess this was not their first time experiencing a tornado. It was quickly over, and we emerged from the basement to find very little damage and continued our picnic. I hate storms. In May, I think, the producers of the Mac-Haydn did call and offered me a show to direct, *The Student Prince*, for the upcoming summer. I was thrilled to accept their offer, and I will always be grateful to Lynn and Linda for taking a chance on me and giving me my first break as a director. As the years went on, I was offered more shows to direct per season. Eventually, I would direct/choreograph a majority of the shows in the season. Although I didn't always agree artistically with the producers, our professional relationship would last fourteen years. I directed some talented performers at the Mac-Haydn, some whom I would later hire at other theatres. And I had the pleasure of working with Muriel Faxon whom I adore, and I appreciate her work with me on the many shows we did together.

CHAPTER 23

1981: AIDS Raises
Its Ugly Head

IT ALL STARTED in 1980, when the first case of Kaposi's sarcoma was diagnosed in San Francisco. Then in 1981, the Center for Disease Control identified the strange new disease as AIDS. It wasn't much later that men of the gay community started to get sick. It usually was a peculiar pneumonia. Also, there seemed to be an epidemic of hepatitis. Soon scientists would discover the HIV virus that causes AIDS. The virus was passed from person to person via the blood. It was also thought and now known that it can spread through unprotected sex.

John took on a new job in the tourism industry. Although John was based in New York City, the home office was in Florida. His new company would require him to have a blood test. Since we were in a monogamous relationship for 10 years, we were not worried. Unfortunately, John did test positive for the HIV virus. Both of us were in shock. I thought at that time that this was the worst day of my life because there was no cure, just death. As it turned out it wasn't the worst day of my life. The worst days were yet to come.

I could only assume that I was also infected. So I did have an HIV test. It was an anxious week of waiting for the results. Finally, my results came back to the clinic, and my test was negative. Thank God, but how? How could one of us test positive and the other negative? Every year when I have my physical checkup, I am tested for all STDs, sexually transmitted diseases, and my test results are always negative. John and I went to The Gay Men's Health Clinic and proceeded to create our wills and our medical directives naming each other executive. Fortunately, John was able to get his former job back along with his health insurance. He immediately found a doctor who was specializing in HIV. His doctor prescribed AZT, the only option at the time. This drug was not a cure. But it was all that they had at the time, and the medical industry was desperate. Many years later, a combination of several drugs was found to successfully reduce the viral load and keep patients who were infected healthy and alive. This is referred to as the Cocktail. John took excellent care of his body and his health. He went to the gym every day, and I cooked almost everything we ate, all very healthy and from scratch. And he was healthy for four and one-half years. Then it all changed.

I am a little foggy on exactly when it all changed, but I think it was soon after John and I went to Palm Springs to visit our friends Mick and Tim. Mick and I had been close friends since 1969. John and I discussed sharing the news about John's test results. The first day in Palm Springs we were all sitting in the den overlooking the beautiful patio and pool catching up when John's pill timer went off. John stood up to retrieve his pill container in the other room, and at the same time Tim's timer went off, and he stood up to do the same. As they left the room Mick and I looked at each other and said something like "Oh no!"

This was the first of many visits with Mick and Tim in Palm Springs and Los Angeles. They commuted back and forth because they worked in L.A. Mick had a successful career as a performer who appeared on television and on stage. He performed in Ann-Margret's and Florence Henderson's nightclub acts. Mick made a successful transition from performer to commercial agent in Hollywood. Sadly, Tim lost his battle with AIDS and passed away.

At some point, John had a medical procedure where they implanted a catheter to make it easier and less abrasive to medicate himself. After he got home from the hospital, I had to go to St. Louis to do a Marvin Hamlisch concert, so John went to Palm Springs to stay with our friends Mick and his new partner, Michael. I called the afternoon I arrived in St. Louis and John answered the phone. I knew immediately that something was wrong. He said he didn't know who I was or where he was. My heart stopped. I didn't know how to react—was he joking with me? No, I knew he wasn't because I could hear in his voice that he was scared. Oh my God, please help me help him. I knew not to panic and to stay calm so I wouldn't scare John. But I was really scared like I had never been in my life. What was happening? I sat down and caught my breath and explained to John who I was and that he was at Mick and Michael's home. Unfortunately, Mick and Michael had gone to the airport to fly somewhere, and John was alone. He said that he had gone to the bedroom where he was staying and saw a wallet. When he opened the wallet he didn't recognize the picture or the name. I didn't know if he was safe or not and somehow I had to get to him. Even if I could leave immediately for the airport and fly to Palm Springs, it would be hours before I could get there. I called his mom who lived about an hour away and told her what was going on and that she needed to get to John, ASAP. Thank God I was able to reach Mick on the phone. I explained to him what was going on and he called his neighbor, whom John had met, and asked him to go over and be with John until his mom arrived. When his parents got there, they took John to the hospital. He was severely dehydrated, and his electrolytes were out of whack. Two days later we were finally able to get John home to me in New York City. Gradually his memory did come back into focus. Thank God this nightmare was over.

We moved from Brooklyn to midtown Manhattan. John had found an apartment that was just a few blocks from the hospital where his doctor was on staff. A couple of days after John came home, he called his doctor and told her what happened in Palm Springs. An MRI was ordered. The results showed that there were two lesions on his brain. His doctor ordered John to check into the hospital ASAP for further tests. John was checked in on the Thursday before Labor Day. His first day of chemo was on Friday. We also found out that what happened in Palm Springs was a reaction from one of his drugs. After Labor Day, a chest X-ray showed that his lungs were compromised. Now that John was going to be in the hospital for a while, my schedule changed. I would wait for him to have his breakfast, and after I fed the kitties, Mary and Dixie, and myself, I would go over to the hospital to spend the day with John. Then late in the afternoon I would come home to take care of the kitties, and then back to the hospital for the rest of the evening. I recall a particular time when I exited the elevator and headed to John's room. I saw John sitting in a chair at the end of the hall. He was writing a letter to his sister, who was living in Australia, that he probably would not see her again. When John read what he had written, I could hear in John's voice that he knew he was probably not going to live much longer. It was a heartbreaking moment for both of us.

Lots of friends came to visit John. Some came every day like our friends Dennis, Frankie, Debbie, and Alan. One day our friends Albert and John came to visit, and when they left, I walked them to the elevator and that's when they offered to provide a private nurse for John. We were overwhelmed by their generosity and it took some strain and stress off of me. Then the day came when his doctor came into his room and told John that he had fought a hard war for several years, but this time he was going to lose the battle. The tears started to pour down his face. I got in bed with him and held him for a while, and he talked about what a wonderful life he'd had and about all the great places where he got to model. He thanked me for loving him and taking care of him.

After some time he said I should go home to take care of the kitties. I said I would come back after his dinner.

Later that night before I headed back to the hospital, I received a call to tell me that John had left the hospital. They said that the police had been alerted. His hospital roommate said that John told him that he was going home. Also, he left in his hospital gown. This wave of panic washed over me. I ran out of the apartment and started running through the neighborhood to find him. Then it suddenly occurred to me that I should go back home and wait for him. Also, I needed to be by the phone. Soon the hospital did call to tell me he was back in his room. The police found him in front of Lincoln Center. I think he was headed to our first apartment on the Upper West Side. He must have forgotten that we'd moved into a new apartment in midtown. I ran to the hospital, and when I walked out of the elevator on his floor, I saw some people in suits waiting for me. They informed me that tomorrow John was being moved to a private room and a guard would be placed outside of his room. It was later that night that his lungs collapsed. Immediately a team of doctors rushed into his room and told me that I should leave. The doctors started to administer anesthesia at the same time they had to cut into his chest so they could insert tubes to reinflate his lungs. I think that was the process. I have never heard screams of unbearable pain like the screams from John. As soon as they could, they administered morphine for the pain. I was finally able to come back into John's room to find him with a tube coming out of each lung. Everything went downhill from there.

The hospital put a cot in John's room for me so I could spend the nights. When he went to sleep, I would sit and watch him and pray as I had never prayed before. My prayer was that John would recover so they could remove the tubes, and I could take him home. He asked a couple of times if I could take him home. I asked his doctor, who said it would be risky. John also asked if I could take him outside so he could listen to the birds. I had to say no. I had never said no to John.

As his pain was increasing, John told me that his doctor promised him that he would never have to be in any pain. So when the pain became unbearable, I would call for the nurse and they would increase his morphine drip. At some point, he did slip into a coma. I don't remember how long he was in the coma. Because he was young, his heart was healthy, even though the rest of his body was beginning to shut down. I finally accepted the painful reality that John was probably not going home with me ever again. Now when I prayed I prayed that if he was not going to recover, please take him now so he could be at peace. On Friday, September 18 at 5 p.m., he took his last breath and with a big sigh he transitioned over to whatever happens when you die. Then I asked for three doctors to verify that he was dead. He wanted to be cremated, so I had to make damn sure he had left his physical body. When we were alone, I closed his eyes and kissed him good-bye.

Pretty much the same group of friends would come to visit John around five in the afternoon. As they arrived, I don't think anyone expected to find that John had just passed away. After everyone had paid their respects, they left so I could have some time alone with John. I kissed him good-bye again and with tears pouring, I realized that I would never see him again. I gathered his things into his gym bag and said, "OK. Let's go home, John." When the kitties saw me walk into the apartment with John's bag, I could tell by the way they looked at me and the bag that they knew John was not coming home.

When our friends who were at the hospital arrived at the apartment, they had food and vodka in hand. So we drank and ate and talked about John for a few hours. Finally, the last guest left, and I made the necessary phone calls to his family and friends. Suddenly, I was faced with my biggest fear—abandonment. I was alone. My best friend would never come home again. Then I cried myself to sleep, which I would do for months to come. The next day started with more crying. When John died he was very thin and looked like he was 90 years old.

I wanted to remember John as if he had never gotten sick. So, I took many of his tear sheets from his portfolio and put them around the apartment. Tear sheets are pages torn out of magazines with ads that he modeled for; these were tools for getting other gigs.

I would try to remember all the good things that we experienced together, like our cross-country trip, which was an exciting experience. There was an afternoon in the hospital when John just out of the blue started to sing to me "Mr. Bojangles"; this really made me smile. Facing the end of his life, he sang me a song. Shortly after his death, I was in our closet and I suddenly realized that I could smell John's body scent in his shirts. It was so comforting and I would do this often. Facing the fact that my life had changed was difficult. I couldn't shop for food without breaking down in the aisle of the grocery store. It had been a long time since I had to cook for just myself. I pretty much lived on Chinese.

One of John's tear sheets. This was shot at a famous restaurant in Paris .

There were two beautiful memorials, in New York and Palm Springs. In New York, many people came to the church to share their love for John. Our friend, Broadway composer John Kander who'd provided a private nurse for John, sang and played a song he wrote for his show *Cabaret* titled "Married." It was an extraordinary moment that touched everyone in the church, especially me. In Palm Springs Mick hosted a lovely memorial at his home so the many friends and family who lived in California could come together to share their love for John. There were helium balloons with John's name and the date of his birth and death printed on them. There were also small note cards on which we could write a note to John, and then we tied our individual note cards to our balloons and then sent them to heaven. I will always be so grateful to Mick, who had called me every day for many months. He knew what I was going through and just what to say because his partner Tim had passed over. I don't know what I would have done without his phone calls, his love, and his support.

CHAPTER 24

Someday My Prince
Will Come, Again

AFTER ABOUT SIX months, I felt like I could go back to work and I needed to go back to work. It was time to end my isolation from the rest of the world. Over the years I had established some steady gigs at several theatres where there was work waiting for me. I was grateful for that. A couple of years after John's passing, a very close friend who musical-directed a large number of my shows had been staying with me between his out-of-town gigs. One night he convinced me that it was time for me to get out of the apartment and be around other people and maybe think about dating again. I was nervous about the dating thing and "safe sex"—something I had not experienced yet.

About three years after John's passing I did start to date again. One night I went to this popular club. I was sitting at the bar when this really "hot" guy walked in. As he passed by I gave him a shy look-over. He seemed to be looking for someone and continued walking further into the bar. As I watched him walk away, I thought to myself, *The back is as good as the front.* I decided that I wanted to meet this young man in the tight white jeans. Even though I was following him from a distance, I felt he knew I was stalking him so I backed off and went back to the bar. A moment later I noticed he was ordering a drink at the other end of the bar. So I walked over to introduce myself and get a closer look. I liked what I saw, so I sat next to him at the bar. We had a couple of drinks and talked for a long time. I could tell right away that I liked him. His name is David, and he's from Iowa. He moved to New York to check out the theatre scene. Currently, he was managing a restaurant. He asked what I did for a living. I hesitated a little because I didn't want him to like me because I was a director and might be in a position to give him a job. But then I figured that there's nothing wrong with "networking," so I told him that I was a Broadway veteran and now a director/choreographer.

After a while, we ended up at my apartment. The evening turned very romantic, and we stayed up late with more talking. As it was very early in the morning I asked if he wanted to stay over—something I didn't usually do—and he did. He came over the next night after he finished work, and the night after that, and so on for three months. He would only go to his apartment to get some more clothes. I began making more and more room for him in the closets. We became very close, and David was my new best friend. My affection for David was growing stronger each day, but I was still grieving somewhat. The terrible memories of John's hospitalization would come in waves. Anything that could go wrong for John did go wrong. I felt so sorry for all the pain he had to go through and the awful things that happened to him. Without any warning, some horrific incident would sneak into my thoughts, and the tears would pour. I would apologize, and David would hug me and say, "It's alright." This one time he said something that totally convinced me that he was the person that I wanted to share the rest of my life with; he said: "I have enough room in my heart for both you and John." That's when I knew that God had blessed me for a second time. A few days later we took a day trip out to Long Island. David wanted to show me Port Jefferson. Before he moved to Manhattan, he'd lived in Port Jefferson with friends from Iowa. He also wanted to show me the theatre where he played Joe Hardy in *Damn Yankees*.

On the drive back to Manhattan, I suggested that since he was basically living with me, we should make it official. I asked, "Do you want to move in permanently and share my home?" A few seconds later he asked me to pull over to this gas station. Without a word he got out of the car and shut the door. I thought to myself, *Is that a no?* David went to a pay phone, and just minutes later he returned to the car. Once inside the car he said, "I just called Ted"—his roommate at the time—"and told him that I was moving in with you."

David had a second job along with managing the restaurant. He would go to shopping malls and track shoppers shopping. The weekend he moved in he was sent to Philadelphia to track shoppers. He went down on a Friday, and I came down on that Saturday. Before we went to dinner, I took a greeting card out of my backpack and handed it to David. Inside the card was a key. The card said something like, *This is a key to my heart and it will also open the door to your new home.*

Once David moved in we started nesting. We mostly stayed home and cooked. Occasionally, we would go out to a restaurant. We were not very social in the beginning, so David had not met most of my friends. I remember one day we were walking down the street when this young actor who'd just worked for me walked up to say hello. I introduced him to David, and we had a brief conversation. After he left, David said, "Don't you have any friends your age?" I thought for a second and replied, "Yes, but most of them have passed away. I guess it's time to stop hogging you for myself and introduce you to my friends."

I spent most of the summer directing and choreographing, mostly at the Mac-Haydn Theatre. On Fridays, after work, David would join me for the weekend. He would take the train up along the Hudson River to Chatham, New York. On Sunday, late afternoon, I would take him back to the train station for his trip back home. As per my contract, the producers had provided me with a car and housing during my employment. The accommodation was a cute little cottage on a horse farm with a stream out back. David and I would take drives into the country on my time off, which was on Saturday and Sunday afternoons. This one afternoon we stopped at a yard sale and bought a picnic table and a Weber barbeque set. What a find! We would also make stops at the country farmers' roadside stands and buy fresh, just gathered vegetables. Since we now had a barbeque set, we would go to the local butcher for steaks or chicken, and we would barbeque the whole weekend and eat at our picnic table.

Since the day we met, David has seen every production that I have directed. In the fall I went to Rock Island, Illinois, to direct and choreograph for a dear friend, Denny Hitchcock, for whom I had directed several shows. I was directing a production of *Grease*. Of course, David was there with me for the opening night, just before Thanksgiving.

It was our first Thanksgiving together, and David's family lived in Iowa, about an hour or so from Rock Island. David thought this would be a good time for me to meet his family, and so I did. And of course, they welcomed me with open arms. David is from a large family: two sisters, two brothers, and his mom who looked like Celeste Holmes. Unfortunately, his dad and another brother had passed on. His mom was sweet enough to let me contribute my momma's cornbread sausage dressing to the Thanksgiving dinner. Later that weekend his family came to see my production of *Grease*. I think they were impressed.

When I was home and not out in the country somewhere directing, David and I enjoyed entertaining. I love to cook, and David likes helping me. I enjoy teaching him how to cook. We learned to work harmoniously in our small kitchen and shared a lot of delicious food with a lot of friends. Oh yes, I want to go back to David liking to help. David is the kind of person who goes out of his way to help anyone who needs help. That's just who he is as a person and just one of his wonderful qualities.

David and I also enjoyed traveling. We would visit New Orleans many times. The first time we went to New Orleans I showed him every block of the French Quarter. We took a streetcar up St. Charles Avenue to the Garden District. Many antebellum homes create the atmosphere of this affluent neighborhood. In the Garden District, you will find the beautifully lush Audubon Park and Zoo. Its borders are the Mississippi River on the south and Tulane University on the north.

We drove up the Mississippi River Road, north of the city, and toured the beautiful plantations. I believe that only 12 survived the war. One of the plantations we visited offered their guests a cold mint julep. It was David's first mint julep, and he loved it. While we were in New Orleans, I took him to my old neighborhood where I grew up. He met my older brother Timmy and his family and my little brother, Randy.

I introduced David to his first roast-beef poor boy. In New Orleans, it's called a po'boy and is the quintessential sandwich of New Orleans. Another New Orleans tradition is barbeque shrimp. Barbeque shrimp is not barbequed on a grill. It's cooked in the oven. Serve with a lot of French bread to dunk into the sauce—yummy! Over the years we have enjoyed the best cuisine at the best restaurants in New Orleans. I took him to an area called West End, located west of the city and on Lake Pontchartrain. Some of the best seafood restaurants are located in the West End. They are on stilts out over Lake Pontchartrain and have many screened windows so you can enjoy the lake breeze. They served the best seafood in the world, right out of the lake. David loved New Orleans, and we would visit many times through the years. Our friend Sandy, who I mentioned earlier, lives in the Quarter and would open her home to us as did our friends Mousey and Leo.

I remember the time I was in Dallas or Houston doing *Irene*, and we had a three-day weekend off. I hadn't been home for a few years, so I planned a trip to New Orleans. I had recently been spending time with another cast member, Merilee, whom I am very fond of. I asked if she had ever been to New Orleans and she said yes, once, so I invited her to join me. I took her all over the Quarter. I took her to Jonny's for a roast-beef po'boy, which turned out not to be the best way to break our three-day fast. Marilee loved her po'boy anyway. I think on our first night we enjoyed dinner in the lovely courtyard of The Court of Two

Sisters—delicious! I also showed her Le Petit Theatre. And of course, I took her to Pat O'Brien's for a Hurricane. Before we left New Orleans, we went to my daddy's house and enjoyed a crawfish feast; Marilee said it was amazing! We did have a good time! As they say in New Orleans, "Laissez les bon temps rouler." Let the good times roll!

CHAPTER 25

From Director/Choreographer to Artistic Director

IN THE EARLY weeks of 2000, I was hired to direct/choreograph an Off-Broadway musical titled *Dressing Room*. This was a backstage musical about the actors in a play and what goes on behind the scenes and in the dressing rooms. The play opened in April at the Soho Playhouse in New York City. The show ran only a few months before closing.

Shortly after *Dressing Room* closed, I was hired by Bill Castellino to direct/choreograph *A Chorus Line* for Western Michigan's Cherry County Playhouse's 2001 season. I brought my friend Amy to assist me with restaging Michael's original production and play the role of Cassie. The theatre was beautiful and had 1,700 seats. The theatre company was very professional and did everything first-class. The production of *A Chorus Line* was a huge hit, and I was invited to return in 2002 to direct/choreograph *Bye Bye Birdie*. This production starred Priscilla Lopez (Tony Award Winner for *A Day in Hollywood, A Night in the Ukraine* and original cast member of *A Chorus Line*) and Jim Walton (Broadway veteran of more than a dozen shows). My friend Amy was now my Associate Choreographer.

Opening Night of *Dressing Room*
From the left is Ronald, David, Sandy, and me.

Early in the spring of 2003, the president, Pam Gallina, of Western Michigan's Cherry County Playhouse, a new position, offered me the Artistic Director's position. In my first season as Artistic Director, we produced *Oklahoma* starring Sandy Duncan, *Barnum* starring Peter Scolari, *Guys and Dolls* starring Eddie Mecca, and *Chicago* starring John Davidson.

Even though the season was very successful, the Board decided to shut down the theatre company. This was due to failed negotiations with the theatre owners and some financial difficulties. I was really bummed out! I enjoyed being the artistic director, and I knew that I did a good job. It was on the plane ride back to New York when I decided that I was done with freelancing as a director/choreographer. Now that I knew I could take charge as an artistic director and successfully produce a season, it was time to have my own theatre company. When I got back home, I told David about my decision to start my own theatre company, and since he shared my passion for theatre, I asked if he would be the managing director. This theatre company would be our family business.

David had a full-time job and I needed to still direct, so we would work on the company on weekends. We filed for and received a 501c3 classification from the IRS. We decided on a name for the company along with a logo to represent the company. Next, we put together a Board of Directors, all very capable and happy to serve. Then we picked a couple of popular musicals as possible considerations for a season and worked up a budget for these shows—a budget for a large musical, medium-sized musical, and a small musical. We now had a theatre company with a name, Premier Performing Arts. Next came a business plan and a budget. Now the company needed a website, which David would create. Once we published the website, we started to raise funds from family and friends along with submitting requests for grants to foundations and sponsorships from corporations.

Of course, we needed a theatre where we would produce our shows. I would often dream about owning our own theatre. We didn't have the money to buy one, but I knew if I found a theatre for sale, somehow we could acquire it. I spent a lot of time online looking for a theatre for sale. I found a nice theatre for sale in California. There were several photos on this listing so I could tell that this theatre might work for us. It was built as a vaudeville and movie theatre. I called the realtor and asked a lot of questions and sent him to the company's website so he could read the company's mission statement and our plan for producing professional musical theatre. I showed the listing to David and shared the info I got from the realtor, and we made an appointment to tour this theatre. We flew out to California and took a tour of the theatre. Unfortunately, the theatre was not suitable for large Broadway musicals. We flew to Ohio to see another theatre, but the stage was too small. We then rented a car and drove to the middle of Pennsylvania to check out yet another theatre. Nothing that we saw suited our needs.

I wasn't giving up. On the drive back to New York, I remembered that a couple of years ago I came across a theatre in Westchester County. At the time it looked as though it was inactive, which was a shame. A few years later I was offered a job to choreograph a show at the very same theatre. During the rehearsal period, I kept looking around the theatre, and I had a good feeling about maybe someday I could produce some musicals here. It was old and needed some work, but the bones were good. When we got home from the Pennsylvania trip, I contacted the management of the theatre in Westchester County and expressed interest in producing in their theatre. They were very interested in our plans, and we discussed the rental agreement, which was all-inclusive. The "all-inclusive" part really worked for us. We now had a possible theatre, The Tarrytown Music Hall in Tarrytown, New York. I then called a friend, Chloe, with whom I had done a couple of shows. I really liked Chloe, and we worked well together. She is a fantastic musical director and conductor. So I figured she would be a wonderful asset to the company. She was thrilled with the idea of working with us. So now the company had a name, Premier Performing Arts, also a staff of three, a Producing Artistic Director, Managing Director, and Musical Director, and a theatre where we could produce our musicals, The Tarrytown Music Hall.

CHAPTER 26

2008: The Economy Crashes and Our First Season Goes with It

IN 2008, WE started planning our first season. The first show was *Plaid Tidings*, a Christmas spinoff from the popular *Forever Plaid*. The first thing I did was to secure the licensing rights. Then I put together a marketing plan and advertising campaign. One of our board members and now a good friend, Janet, was a graphic artist who created a company logo, posters, and fliers for the show. We took these fliers and posters and canvased the Westchester communities. We produced a radio commercial and sold ads for the *Playbill* program. In September we started casting and hired a group of really talented actors/singers. Then I placed a bond with Actor's Equity to ensure two weeks of salary for the cast. I hired a set designer, lighting designer, and stage manager. We also put a deposit on the theatre rental. Everything was going so well, and I was really enjoying this producing thing again. Then in November, just three weeks before the first rehearsal was to start, the economy turned upside down. Ticket sales were slow, which made us nervous. We had a meeting with the Board of Directors to discuss what we should do. In light of what was happening, the Board suggested that we should consider canceling the season. We were devastated but agreed with the Board that it was the best thing. Two years of a lot of "blood, sweat, and tears" along with hard work just went down the drain. I made the necessary phone calls to the cast and others. They were understandably disappointed but supported our decision.

When the shock wore off, the depression settled in—in a big way. For the first time we did not put up a Christmas tree nor did we celebrate the holidays. David and I did, however, vow not to shut down the company but to move forward in the new year. The idea of producing professional theatre and our mission statement was still a viable one; Premiere Performing Arts would offer much-needed employment to the unemployed and underemployed theatrical community. So the day after New Year's we continued to move forward.

David still had his day job, and I continued to direct from time to time. I was hired to direct and choreograph a production of *Urinetown* in New Jersey. It was a show that I had not directed before, which excited me. As the show developed during the rehearsal period, I kept thinking that this material is excellent. Once the show was blocked out and the musical numbers staged, I scheduled run-through rehearsals of the show, scene by scene. Every day I was convinced that this show was good—better than good, it was terrific. I got it right. It turned out to be one of my favorite shows that I have directed and choreographed. The whole show just evolved out of my clear understanding of what the creators intended and how to tell their story. One of the actors in the show introduced me to her parents on opening night, and they just happened to be successful Broadway producers, Jay and Cindy Gutterman. During the run of the show I noticed that her parents attended every performance. On the last performance, I went up to her mother who was sitting in the lobby before the show. I walked over to her and said, "What a great mom you are for coming to every performance." And she replied it was because she loved my production. Then I said, "Why don't you and your husband produce the show as a Broadway revival?" She responded that they were talking about that very thing. I said, "Would you consider me directing the show?" And she said, "Of course, it's your show that gave us the idea." I remember our conversation word for word because this was a moment in my career that I would never forget. These two very experienced Broadway producers entrusting me with their Broadway show. With that said, the bell rang indicating the show was starting. As she went into the theatre, I went outside to call David to share the news that I just might be directing/choreographing my first Broadway show. After a few months, the producers informed me that the owners of the rights were not ready to release them at this time. Oh well, it may still happen.

URINETOWN CAST

CHAPTER 27

Focusing on the Theatre Company

IT SEEMED THAT when I had to leave town to direct, nothing would happen with the company. David had a full-time job to focus on, and I couldn't turn down a directing gig. But I had to make a decision between directing and producing. I decided to put the directing career on hold and put all my energy into Premier Performing Arts. We participated in a lot of the street fairs in the area, passing out fliers to whoever would pass by our table. If they stopped, we would go into our song and dance about how we planned to bring Broadway to Tarrytown. We did the necessary networking by attending many of the businesses' afternoon get-togethers. We participated with the Chamber of Commerce. We did everything we could to make Premier Performing Arts' presence known in the Westchester communities. A great deal of time was spent on the train to and from Tarrytown.

I spent my days researching foundations and corporations that offered grants and donations to not-for-profit theatre companies. After hours of refining my search to those that might have an interest in our company, I usually would end up with approximately 35 possibilities. I would use a template that a professional grant writer made for us when we first started our company. I would fashion the grant request to fit the foundation or corporation's guidelines. Every foundation had their unique requirements. It would take a couple of weeks to write a grant, then tweak it a few times before it was ready for submitting. Most foundations don't accept unsolicited grants, so you send those foundations a letter of inquiry.

The whole process of fundraising was long and complicated. It could take about two or more months to create a different letter for each foundation or corporation, print them, and mail them. Then you would follow up with a phone call, and usually, you only got the voice mail. So you waited and hoped someone would contact you with an interest in your mission. At some of the classes we took on grant writing and fundraising for nonprofits, we learned that most foundations did not grant to new companies without a history; their money was already committed. You just have to continue to submit year after year and pray your turn would come. It was very frustrating, but I knew there was a need for Premier Performing Arts and my idea for this theatre company was still viable.

So we needed to produce something and create a history for the company. I decided on a fundraising concert which would be affordable for the company. Our friend Chloe was very close to the Menken family. She approached Alan Menken about doing a fundraiser for the theatre company and he agreed. I asked some of my friends who were Broadway veterans to perform, and our neighbor across the hall, Alex, who coached and accompanied many celebrities, asked some of his associates to join in the fundraising concert. Everyone agreed and volunteered their time and talents. The concert was titled *Broadway Tonight with Alan Menken and Friends.* The friends were Broadway luminaries like Lee Roy Reams, Anita Gillette, Penny Fuller, Harvey Evans, Penny Worth, Kurt Peterson, the late Victoria Mallory, John Tracey Egan, Joel Martin's Jazzical, and the Nunziata Twins.

A friend of ours, Tom Capolla, who was helping with marketing for the concert, offered to approach Valerie Smaldone about being the Mistress of Ceremonies. Ms. Smaldone is a popular host, interviewer, and entertainer. We were thrilled when she agreed.

My generous and very talented friend, Bebe Neuwirth, prerecorded a phone call to wish us the best and pitch our theatre company to the audience at this concert. At a particular time, I pretended my cell phone was vibrating, and I took it out of my pocket and pretended that Bebe was actually calling. I then put my cell phone by the mic and the sound guy would play Bebe's prerecorded message. It sounded like she was live on my phone. She was funny and a perfect ambassador for the company. Anyway, the concert was a success, and some of our friends, led by our dear friend Jimmy Ashmore, volunteered to sell the performers' CDs in the lobby of the theatre. There was a meet-and-greet after the concert along with a champagne toast for the cast and guests in the balcony lobby. After the bills were paid the company did raise some money, but not enough to produce a musical production.

The following spring the company planned a Sunday afternoon Cocktail Garden Reception to raise money and create interest in Premier Performing Arts within the community. We bought a mailing list of people in the area who liked theatre and mailed out about a hundred-plus invites with R.S.V.P. envelopes. We ended up with maybe 60 guests. One of our board members, Mary, offered her beautiful home in Sleepy Hollow, New York, which overlooked the Hudson River. Instead of just serving wine with cheese and crackers, we decided to go first class with this fundraiser. We invited Sandy Duncan to be our guest host. She was charming and funny and spoke about the importance of the theatre in the community. She was the perfect host to represent Premier Performing Arts. The reception was catered by friends who owned a catering company in New York City. They offered up delicious appetizers that were served by our friends Alec Timerman and Mary Lou Barber, both of them successful professional theatre performers. They were great at promoting Premier Performing Arts as they allured the guests with the luscious food and fabulous signature cocktail mixed by Alec.

As the reception ended, the guests were handed a canvas tote bag with the company's logo, PPA, Premier Performing Arts, on the front. Inside was information on the company like our Mission Statement, the upcoming season, and how to support Premier Performing Arts, including a self-addressed stamped envelope for donations. Although we did receive some donations, it was not enough to support the budget for a musical. Next we put together another fundraiser; it was a barbeque in honor of Premier Performing Arts. Jimmy Ashmore offered his building's rooftop party space, which was perfect.

I believe it was the end of that summer that the Board of Directors' two-year service had expired. They were wonderful and participated at all the events. David and I miss them.

I continued writing grants, although I knew that unless we were invited to submit a grant proposal, chances of receiving a grant were slim. In 2016, we did eventually receive a phone call from a representative of a foundation. She invited the company to submit a grant proposal. With that said, I did send a formal grant proposal. We did not receive the grant this time, but we were encouraged to continue submitting a grant request.

CHAPTER 28

Same-Sex Marriage

IN JUNE OF 2011, the State of New York legalized same-sex marriage. In June 2011, David and I flew to Chicago to meet up with his sister Janice and her son John at the airport. We were going to drive to Dubuque, Iowa, to surprise their mom with a birthday party, only her birthday was not until August. They figured the only way to really surprise her was to have the party in June. That should work. Anyway, we were driving from Chicago to Dubuque; Janice was the driver. About an hour into the drive I saw this big sign on the side of the highway that said "WELCOME TO WISCONSIN." I said, "Why are we going to Wisconsin?" At which time Janice turned the car around and headed toward Dubuque.

After this diversion, we frequently checked the cell phone GPS to make sure we were on track. One of those checks was interrupted by a notification that New York state had just legalized same-sex marriage right before the Gay Pride celebration in New York City. Wow! Now, David and I had discussed getting married if New York ever legalized it. Since we had been living together for fourteen years, did we need to get married? There are many benefits to marriage. So jokingly, I proposed to

David in the backseat of this rental car. How unromantic. Of course, he said yes! Then I thought, how ironic—here we are driving down this highway in the dark Iowa night and back home the gay community is celebrating Gay Pride Week along with Same-Sex Marriage.

What a party we were missing! Oh well, this trip was for David and Janice's mom, and it will make her really happy, and that means a lot because soon she will be my mother-in-law. Three words I never thought I would say. His mom was surprised and happy to hear about the engagement. There were lots of guests, and everyone congratulated us on our engagement. I don't know how many people asked if we had picked the big date yet. A good time was had by all!

After living together for 17 years, David and I were finally married in 2014. We started planning our wedding reception, but after months of searching for the perfect venue and coordinating dates between families, the planning came to a halt. As time was of the essence, we decided to go downtown to the courthouse to get married. No, no one was pregnant! I was anxious to have David's name added to my lease on our apartment. Because the apartment is rent stabilized, the only way his name would be added to the lease was if we were legally married. Well, now his name is on the lease, and if something happens to me, David will not lose his home.

When we arrived at the courthouse to get married the lobby was buzzing with happy people, all there for the same reason. David made an interesting observation when he said: "All the people here are smiling and happy, whereas, in the courthouse down the block the people are not smiling as they wait to see if they will have to serve on a jury." Our good friend Paul Kravitz was our witness. The whole ceremony took less than one minute.

CHAPTER 29

My Retirement

GOING BACK A few years to July 2011, I celebrated my 65th birthday and started receiving my pensions from the theatrical unions where I am a member. And moving ahead to 2016, I celebrated my 50th anniversary in show business—a milestone for anybody who survives that long in show business. I'm blessed to have made a living at my chosen occupation doing what I love to do. And I'll tell you what: the best thing about turning 70 is collecting my Social Security.

At the end of 2017, I officially retired. This is something I never thought I would ever consider—I love the career I created. After all those years of performing strenuous dancing and tumbling, both resulting in two surgeries, my body has been sorely compromised. I now deal with arthritic pain in my knee and spinal stenosis. At the beginning of 2017, it became excruciating just getting to work and back home. There were too many times that it was impossible. Just walking one or two blocks was agonizing. God bless my husband, who would take on most of the daily chores that were and still are too painful for me. So, as a result, I quit my part-time job of fundraising for The New York City Ballet and officially retired at the end of 2017. I do miss the people I worked with

Nancy, our manager. There are some talented people and some interesting people who worked in that room. I enjoyed the few comp tickets I received while working there, and David and I enjoyed having a subscription to the NYC Ballet. I love sitting in the theatre and vicariously dancing with the dancers on stage. It's wonderful remembering how it felt when I was younger and could dance like that.

I have to tell you, I am loving this retirement thing! I now have all the time in the world to write my memoir. Hopefully, I can remember enough to fill up a book. As I spend my days at the computer putting down my memories, many thoughts cross my mind. I remember hearing someone saying that being a writer could be a lonely experience. Not long into my book I suddenly found myself sharing that experience. Sometimes David could come home for lunch and sometimes he couldn't. I didn't want to eat alone so I would think about who I could call to have lunch with me. That's when I had to face the sad reality that most of my close friends have also retired and have left New York. Or worse, they have passed on, like my friends Debbie Reynolds and Carrie Fisher.

It was shocking when I heard that Carrie had died so suddenly. I knew how much Debbie worried about Carrie and always made sure Carrie was safe and cared for. I called Penny Worth, with whom I did *Irene*, and who was very close to Debbie and Carrie. I wanted to find out if she knew any more than what we were hearing on the news. We both feared that this loss would probably be more than Debbie could take. The day after Carrie departed this world, Debbie followed. Even though we felt that this would happen, we didn't expect it to be so immediate.

The loss of Debbie was really painful. On December 28, 2016, there was one more star in the heavenly skies. I miss them both and will always cherish the wonderful memories.

As I reflect back, I am very grateful to the Universal Mind, God, for all the blessings and miracles that have come into my life. I am thankful to my momma for her love and support of my dream. I am grateful for her trust in me as a young teenager to be on my own in the French Quarter at night, which was when rehearsals and performances happened. Of course, she did worry. I would have never received the encouragement from the critics and audiences to pursue a career in New York City had my momma said, "No, you're too young to be on your own in the Quarter at night."

And I am proud of what I have accomplished to make "my dream" a reality. Not just on Broadway, but including my success in Hollywood with all the television shows and movies that I was able to add to my resume. I have directed/choreographed well over a hundred-plus musicals around the country and in Canada. Because of my association with *A Chorus Line*, I have often been asked to restage Michael Bennett's original production at many theatres. It is always an honor to pass on the legacy that Michael gifted to me and so many other alumni of *A Chorus Line*.

I appreciate having the opportunity to mentor so many young actors who were at the beginning of their careers and then watch them grow into successful performers. I am blessed to have met and worked with so many beautiful people throughout my life and career, all those who are still with us and the many who are not. The theatrical community has mourned the loss of so much talent.

As I began writing this chapter, chapter 29, it began to feel like this would be the last chapter of my book. When I retired, my life changed. For example: I am no longer seeking work. After more than fifty-plus years of auditioning and going to dance classes, voice classes, and acting classes, I no longer have to do that. I no longer have to do any networking and researching the websites of so many theatres to see what shows they would be producing; I no longer have to do that. Nor am I sending my resume to the producers or artistic directors with hopes of adding new theatres to my roster of regular gigs. I can say that is no longer a part of my life. I will, however, happily dust off my director's hat for a project that truly excites me.

I am looking forward to many more years of miracles and blessings along with a healthy and happy life with David. Looking back it's been an awesome journey. And to believe it all began with a childhood dream. A dream that I just could not let go of.